HOW TO BUILD YOUR CREDIT FROM PRISON

ELIJAH R. FREEMAN

URBAN AINT DEAD

CONTENTS

URBAN AINT DEAD
P.O Box 448
Maybrook, NY 12543

Contact Author on FB: Elijah R. Freeman / IG: @the_future_of_urban_fiction

Contact Publisher at www.urbanaintdead.com

Email: urbanaintdead@gmail.com

Print ISBN: 978-1-969593-14-7

STAY UP TO DATE

To stay up to date on new releases, plus get information on contests, sneak peeks and more,

Click the link below...
https://mailchi.mp/6d21003686d1/subscribe

SOUNDTRACKS

Scan the QR Code below to listen to the Soundtracks/Singles of some of your favorite U.A.D titles:

Don't have Spotify or Apple Music?
No Sweat!
Visit your choice streaming platform and search URBAN AINT DEAD.

Currently on lock serving a bid?
JPay, iHeartRadio, WHATEVER!
We got you covered.
Simply log into your facility's kiosk or tablet, go to music and search URBAN AINT DEAD.

URBAN AINT DEAD PRESENTS

Like & Follow us on social media:

FB - URBAN AINT DEAD

IG: @uadpresents

Tik Tok - @uadpresents

Submission Guidelines

Submit the first three chapters of your completed manuscript to urbanaintdead@gmail.com, subject line: Your book's title. The manuscript must be in a .doc file and sent as an attachment. The document should be in Times New Roman, double-spaced, and in size 12 font. Also, provide your synopsis and full contact information. If sending multiple submissions, they must each be in a separate email. Have a story but no way to submit it electronically? You can still submit to URBAN AINT DEAD. Send in the first three chapters, written or typed, of your completed manuscript to:

URBAN AINT DEAD
P.O Box 448
Maybrook, NY 12543

DO NOT send original manuscript. Must be a duplicate.
Provide your synopsis and a cover letter containing your full contact information.
Thanks for considering URBAN AINT DEAD.

DEDICATION

This book is dedicated to Eric Haynes
R.I.P., Playa...

DISCLAIMER

This book is intended for informational and educational purposes only. The author is not a licensed financial advisor, attorney, or credit repair specialist. The strategies, suggestions, and insights shared throughout this book are based on personal experience, research, and general financial principles.

Every individual's financial situation is different, and results may vary. Readers, especially those who are incarcerated, should understand that access to financial tools, communication methods, and resources may be limited and subject to facility rules and regulations.

Nothing in this book should be interpreted as legal or financial advice. Readers are encouraged to consult with qualified professionals and verify all information, especially as it relates to laws such as the Fair Credit Reporting Act (FCRA), which may change over time.

The author and publisher are not responsible for any financial decisions, outcomes, or actions taken based on the information provided in this book.

By reading this book, you acknowledge that you are responsible for your own financial decisions and actions.

Why Credit Matters — Even Behind Bars

"Recognizing your credit status is the first step toward reclaiming your financial freedom, regardless of your current situation."

- Jewel Burks Solomon

Okay, y'all. So, I was thinking to myself what else I could present to y'all to focus on while doing time instead of the normal day-to-day prison bullshit that goes on, and it hit me... credit!

Credit does not operate on emotion. It does not pause because life becomes complicated. It does not care about circumstance, location, or intent. It records behavior and produces consequences. Whether you are active in the financial system or completely disconnected from it, your credit profile continues to exist. That reality alone makes understanding it a necessity, not an option.

For many incarcerated individuals, credit feels distant or irrelevant. But distance does not equal immunity. Financial systems continue to function whether you are participating in them or not. If you do nothing, your credit still evolves — either through aging accounts, accumulating damage, or becoming vulnerable to misuse. The question is not whether credit matters. The question is whether you will manage it intentionally or leave it unattended.

Now, we're three books into our journey of different ways we can boss ourselves up and get on the right track from prison, so if you've read *How To Publish A Book From Prison* and *How To Invest In The Stock Market From Prison,* you already know you're in for some game.

If you're reading this book, you might be asking yourself: What does credit have to do with prison? You're stuck behind the wall, maybe for months or years, with little access to money, jobs, or the outside world. To many incarcerated people, credit seems like something that only matters on the "outside", something for bankers, businesspeople, or big cities. "I'll worry about that when I get out," you might tell yourself.

But here's the straight drop truth, no cut: Whether you're locked up for now or counting down the days to freedom, your credit matters. Your credit history is your financial reputation. It follows you wherever you go, no matter where you live or work, even in prison. While you may not use credit cards, buy a home, or get a car loan while incarcerated, the decisions you make today can build a foundation for your future.

Let me break it down for you:

1. Your Life After Release Depends On It

When you walk back into the world, you'll need somewhere to live, a way to get around, and maybe even a job. Landlords check credit reports before renting out apartments. Employers sometimes run credit checks for certain positions. Buying a car or setting up utilities? Those companies all want to see your credit. If your credit's on the floor (or you have no credit history at all), doors will slam shut. With good credit, you'll have more options, save money, and take back control of your life.

2. Your Credit Record is Permanent

Credit doesn't "take a break" just because you're incarcerated. Old debts, missed payments, and identity theft can keep piling up while you're inside unless you take action. Building and protecting your credit from prison means you're ready to move forward when you get out, not starting from behind. That's what you don't want to do. Playin' catch up to people who had surplus years of a head start on you can be frustrating and has been known to cause many to crash out. Don't put yourself in that predicament.

3. You Don't Have To Wait Until Release

People often believe they need a job, a house, or a big bank balance to start building credit. But with determination and the right tools, you can start repairing or building your credit, even from a cell. Every letter you mail, every step you take matters. Even small actions will make a difference in your score.

4. Building Credit is Building Hope

Incarceration can take away your choices, but managing your credit is one thing you can control. Every positive mark on your credit report brings you closer to freedom, stability, and independence. It's an investment in your future, your dignity, and your ability to start over.

So, why work on your credit while you're in prison?

Because your past doesn't have to define your future. Because you deserve a second chance. Because rebuilding your credit is about more than numbers; it's about reclaiming your life.

"Success is not final, failure is not fatal: it is the courage to continue that counts."

—Winston S. Churchill

You have the courage. This book will show you the steps. Your journey begins now.

The Role Credit Plays In Housing, Jobs, Utilities, and Financial Independence

When you hear the word "credit", you might think it only matters if you want a loan or a credit card. But the truth is, your credit affects almost every part of your life when you get out: where you live, where you work, and how you survive day to day. Let's make it simple and break down exactly how credit matters in real life.

Credit and Housing

Want an apartment when you get out? Most landlords check your credit report before they rent to you. They want to see if you pay your bills on time and if you have debts you haven't paid back. If your credit is bad or you don't have any credit history, landlords might turn you down or ask for extra money up front, like a big deposit.

If you ever want to buy a house, your credit score is even more important. Banks use it to decide if they'll give you a mortgage, how much interest you'll pay, and whether they'll trust you with a loan at all. Good credit means better chances of getting approved and paying less money over time.

Credit and Jobs

Some employers look at your credit report before hiring you, especially for jobs where you handle money, work in security, or deal with private information. They don't want to hire someone who looks irresponsible with their finances.

If your credit report shows old debts, missed payments, or collections, some employers may think twice. Even if you're hardworking and honest, bad credit can make it harder to get certain jobs. Good credit tells employers you're responsible and can be trusted.

Credit and Utilities

When you get out, you'll need electricity, gas, water, maybe even internet or phone service. Utility companies often check your credit before signing you up. If you have bad credit or no credit, they might ask for a deposit (a big chunk of money up front just to turn on your lights). Good credit can save you that expense, making it easier to settle into your new life.

Credit and Financial Independence

Credit isn't just about borrowing money. It's about freedom. With good credit, you can:

- Get approved for credit cards to help cover emergencies or build your score even higher

- Qualify for better interest rates, saving money every time you borrow

- Have more choices — where you live, work, and how you pay for things

- Start a business more easily, if that's your dream

- Use your financial reputation to get what you need, without relying on others

Bad credit ties your hands. It can keep you stuck, struggling and depending on loans with high interest, asking friends or family for help, or always scrambling to make extra payments.

Credit Is a Tool, Not a Trap

Credit doesn't care about your past mistakes or why you ended up in prison. It just records how you handle your money. The good news is you can change it — by paying bills on time, clearing up old debts, and learning what steps to take, even from behind the wall.

When you understand credit, you can use it to open doors. You'll have a better shot at safe housing, decent jobs, reliable utilities, and the independence to live how you choose.

Take control of your credit now so you can take control of your life when you're free. The effort you put in today isn't just for a number on a page; it's for the life you want to live tomorrow.

J.A.I.L. — Just Another Inmate Lie

When you're incarcerated, it's easy to hear (and believe) stories about credit that simply aren't true. But let's be real… *niggas be cappin'*. These myths can lead you astray and even sabotage your efforts to build a better future. Let's clear the air and tackle every common misconception so you know exactly what's fact and what's fiction.

Myth #1: Your Credit Record Starts Over After Prison

Fact: Prison does not erase your credit history. Your credit report is a record of your financial activity, not your criminal activity. Old debts, missed payments, and defaults remain on your credit report for years, even if you've been incarcerated. Nothing gets automatically wiped clean due to time served or your release date. The credit bureaus don't even know you're locked up right now. If so, scammers using incarcerated people's names and socials to do tax fraud would've never been a thing... but it was.

<u>Myth #2: Credit Reports Include Your Criminal Record</u>

Fact: Credit reports do not list convictions, prison time, or arrests. These reports focus only on financial matters — loans, credit cards, collections, bankruptcies, and some civil judgments. Employers, landlords, or lenders can't see your criminal history through credit bureaus.

<u>Myth #3: You Can't Build or Fix Credit While In Prison</u>

Fact: While prison does make building credit harder, it is possible to correct errors, dispute fraudulent activity, and even start new positive credit accounts — with help from family, friends, or authorized users. You can mail requests and disputes to the credit bureaus directly from prison.

<u>Myth #4: Old Debts Automatically Vanish After a Few Years</u>

Fact: Most negative entries, like late payments and collections, stay on your report for seven years and bankruptcies for ten. Some debts may become "time-barred" — meaning collectors can't sue to collect — but they still appear on your credit unless you pay or dispute them.

<u>Myth #5: Credit Is Only for Buying Big Things (Houses, Cars, etc.)</u>

Fact: Credit affects much more than just big purchases. It impacts your ability to rent an apartment, get a job, set up utilities, and sometimes even get a cell phone contract.

<u>Myth #6: The Government Will Fix Your Credit When You Get Out</u>

Fact: No government agency automatically repairs your credit upon release. All cleaning up — disputing errors, paying debts, and building positive history — must be done by you or someone on your behalf. There is no "credit forgiveness" program for released prisoners.

Myth #7: If You Don't Use Credit, You Don't Need Good Credit

Fact: Even if you avoid credit cards and loans, your credit score still matters for housing, jobs, utility deposits, and other basic needs. Not having credit can be just as limiting as having bad credit.

Myth #8: Credit Repair Companies Can Instantly "Fix" Your Credit

Fact: Beware of scams! No company can erase accurate negative info or instantly boost your score. Many credit repair services charge high fees for actions you can do yourself — like mailing disputes, negotiating with creditors, and monitoring your credit reports.

Myth #9: You Have to Wait Until Release to Check Your Credit

Fact: You can request your credit reports by mail from prison. AnnualCreditReport.com provides free reports from each major bureau every year. You do not need internet access, just a mailing address and the required documentation.

Myth #10: Authorized User Status Is Risky or Won't Help

Fact: If a trusted family member adds you as an authorized user to their credit card, their positive history can help your score. You aren't responsible for the debt, and you don't need to have physical access to the card.

Myth #11: Collection Accounts Must Be Paid in Full to Be Removed

Fact: You can sometimes negotiate with creditors to pay less than the full amount ("settlement") or arrange a "pay for delete" agreement. Always get these agreements in writing.

Myth #12: You Can't Dispute Credit Errors from Prison

Fact: Disputing errors is your right under the law, and you can do it by mail. Include evidence, like court records or documentation of

your incarceration if relevant. Always send written disputes and keep copies for your records.

Myth #13: Inactivity on Accounts Doesn't Matter

Fact: If you stop using credit cards or accounts, the lender may close them. Closed accounts can reduce your available credit and shorten your credit history, which can hurt your score.

Myth #14: Family or Friends Can Legally Fix Your Credit Without Your Permission

Fact: No one can legally act on your credit without your written authorization (power of attorney, for example). Never share personal info like Social Security numbers unless you trust the person and understand the risks.

Myth #15: Debts Incurred Before Incarceration Can't Affect You After Release

Fact: Unpaid debts, even old ones, can lower your score, result in lawsuits, and be collected after release.

Myth #16: Income is Required to Build Credit

Fact: While income can help you qualify for credit products, you can start by disputing errors, being added as an authorized user, or maintaining older accounts — even from prison.

Myth #17: Bankruptcy Erases All Debts and Instantly Improves Credit

Fact: Bankruptcy is a legal process that can remove or reorganize many debts, but it will remain as a negative mark on your report for up to ten years. Some debts (child support, student loans, certain fines) are not erased.

Myth #18: You Can't Take Control of Your Credit Until You're Released

Fact: You can begin repairing, protecting, and even building credit right now, from where you are. Start by ordering reports, disputing inaccuracies, and planning for your future steps.

Understanding (and rejecting) these myths clears the path for you to take real action. While you may face obstacles unique to incarceration, knowing the truth sets you up to take back control and build a financial future with real opportunities.

Separation of Credit from Criminal Record

When it comes to building or rebuilding your credit, one common misconception is that a criminal record has a direct impact on your credit score. While being incarcerated may indirectly affect your financial standing, it is important to understand that your creditworthiness and your criminal record are two separate entities in the eyes of lenders, credit bureaus, and financial institutions. Again, they know nothing about the fact that you served time. This separation is a key principle to grasp on the journey to improving your financial health.

Understanding Credit Scores and Reports

Your credit score is a numerical representation of your financial history as reported by credit bureaus such as Experian, Equifax, and TransUnion. It factors in elements like:

1. Payment History – Whether you pay your bills on time
2. Credit Utilization – The amount of credit you are using compared to your total available credit
3. Length of Credit History – How long your credit accounts have been active
4. Credit Mix – The variety of credit accounts (e.g., credit cards, loans)
5. New Credit – The number of recent credit inquiries.

Criminal records, including arrests, charges, convictions, or the fact that you were incarcerated, do not appear on credit reports. By law, credit bureaus do not track criminal activity. However, the financial consequences of imprisonment, such as unpaid debts, closed accounts, or delinquencies while incarcerated, can affect your credit history.

Why Criminal Records Don't Affect Credit Directly

Criminal records and credit reports are maintained in completely separate systems. Here's why:

- Credit Bureaus Don't Collect Legal Data: The three main credit bureaus in the U.S. do not include data from the criminal justice system in your credit file. This means a court sentence or time served in prison will not affect your credit score directly.

- Lenders Focus on Financial Behavior: When assessing your credit application, lenders are concerned with your creditworthiness, not your past incarceration. They evaluate your financial behavior over time, which is reflected in your credit report.

However, lenders may still perform background checks as part of their evaluation process. Criminal records can appear there, but this is separate from the credit check. In most cases, responsible credit usage and a strong financial record can outweigh the stigma of a criminal background.

Indirect Ways Prison May Impact Credit

Although incarceration doesn't directly affect your credit, there are indirect ways that your time in prison could damage your financial profile:

1. Missed Payments During Incarceration: If you had existing debts before your incarceration, such as credit cards, car loans, or mortgages, payments may have gone unpaid if no one managed your finances for you. Missed payments can severely damage your credit score.

2. Defaulted Loans: Unpaid loans during prison can lead to defaults, which are reported on credit reports and remain there for up to seven years.

3. Collections and Charge-Offs: If payments go unpaid for too long, creditors may sell the debt to collections agencies, or they might charge off the debt altogether. Both scenarios significantly lower your credit score.

4. Closed Accounts: Creditors may close long-standing accounts due to inactivity, further dwindling your credit portfolio. Accounts with long credit histories are beneficial to your score, so their closure can be damaging.

5. Identity Theft Risk: Prisoners are particularly vulnerable to identity theft, as their financial affairs often go unmanaged for extended periods. If someone uses your credit or steals your identity while

you're incarcerated, the damage to your financial standing could be significant.

It's crucial to manage these financial risks to protect or rebuild your credit while in prison.

Steps to Keep Credit Separate from Legal Record

To ensure that your credit recovery efforts remain unaffected by your criminal record, take these strategic steps.

1. Monitor Your Credit Report: Start by obtaining free annual copies of your credit reports from all three major bureaus (Experian, Equifax, and TransUnion). You can do this through the government-approved website AnnualCreditReport.com. Look for errors, identity theft, or unauthorized activity that may have occurred while you were incarcerated.

2. Address Delinquencies Quickly: If any of your accounts went delinquent during prison, contact the creditors immediately. Explain your situation and try to negotiate repayment terms or settlements.

3. Open a Secure Line of Communication with Creditors: Being in prison makes communication challenging, but setting up authorized representatives or creating a clear channel of correspondence with creditors is essential.

4. Dispute Incorrect Information: Inaccurate reports on your credit file due to unpaid debts or fraudulent activity should be immediately disputed with the credit bureaus. The Fair Credit Reporting Act (FCRA) gives you the right to contest these items.

5. Separate Background Checks from Credit Evaluations: If you're rebuilding from scratch post-incarceration, be prepared to face background checks when applying for certain jobs, housing, or loans. Be transparent about your past but emphasize your progress in managing finances and improving credit.

6. Start Secured Credit Accounts: If your credit score isn't stellar due to financial issues during incarceration, focus on positive rebuilding. Secured credit cards or credit-builder loans can help you earn a good credit score, even if you're starting from rock bottom.

Preparing for Life After Prison

Your credit future depends on the proactive steps you take before and after your release from prison. Having a financial rehabilitation plan is critical. Upon release, ensure you:

- Establish a stable income source to make consistent payments.
- Demonstrate financial responsibility to landlords, creditors, and potential employers.
- Use tools like budgeting apps or financial planners to keep your credit profile on track.

Remember, your credit score does not define your character, nor does it keep a record of your criminal history. It reflects your financial responsibility. By separating emotional stigma from financial recovery, you can create a strong credit foundation for yourself, regardless of your past circumstances. Keep your eyes focused on the ultimate prize — a solid financial future.

The Myth of "Credit Amnesty" After Several Years

One of the most pervasive myths in the world of credit repair is the idea of "credit amnesty" (the belief that after a certain number of years, all negative marks on your credit report will magically disappear and you'll get a fresh start). While there's some truth to the concept that certain types of negative information do eventually fall off your credit report, the reality of the situation is far more complex and often misunderstood.

The Timeframe Misconception

Many people believe that after seven years, all debts and negative credit history are wiped clean. This misconception stems from the rules set by the Fair Credit Reporting Act (FCRA), which stipulates the length of time certain types of information can remain on your credit report. For example:

- Late Payments: Most will remain on your credit report for up to seven years.
- Charge-offs: These fall off after seven years as well.
- Bankruptcies: Chapter 7 bankruptcies typically stay on your report for ten years, while Chapter 13 remains for seven years after the discharge.

- Collections: These drop off seven years after the original delinquency date.

This timeline is not the same as debt forgiveness. Just because a debt no longer appears on your credit report doesn't erase your responsibility to pay it if the creditor is still pursuing it. In some cases, creditors sell old debts to collection agencies, and while the original account may drop off your report, the new collection agency's account could appear.

Activity Can Revive Old Debt

Here's where the myth becomes particularly dangerous: Many people assume old debts are "dead" once a certain amount of time has passed. In reality, certain actions can restart the clock on debt collection efforts. For example, making a payment (even a partial one) or acknowledging the debt in writing can reset the statute of limitations in many states. This doesn't affect the seven-year reporting rule but can extend the period during which creditors can legally sue you to collect the debt.

The Importance of Proactive Credit Repair

Waiting for negative information to simply "expire" is not a strategy for rebuilding credit. Even if an account drops off your credit report, the absence of positive activity (such as on-time payments and responsible credit usage) can limit your progress. Relying on the hope that your credit will magically repair itself once the timeline expires can keep you stuck in a cycle of poor credit.

Exceptions to the Rule

While most negative items do disappear after seven years, some creditors may still pursue debts under different legal circumstances, especially if the debt is tied to unpaid taxes, student loans, or other obligations that have special status under the law.

The Bottom Line

The myth of credit amnesty is a tempting one, especially for people unsure of how to rebuild credit in difficult situations, such as incarceration. It's easy to believe that time alone will fix your credit, but this is rarely the case. Instead, the key to rebuilding your credit (even from prison) is education, strategy, and persistence. By understanding the rules and taking proactive steps to establish positive credit behaviors, you can set yourself on the path to financial recovery and independence, regardless of what your credit report says today.

Understanding Credit

"When you understand credit, you hold the power to build generational wealth. Your credit score is like your adult report card — it reflects how much you value yourself."

- John Hope Bryant

WHAT IS CREDIT?

Credit is an agreement between you and a lender — such as a bank, store, or credit card company. They give you money, goods, or access to services now, and you agree to pay them back later, usually with interest.

Credit is a structured system. It is not personal. It is mathematical. Lenders do not evaluate your intentions; they evaluate your history. They rely on patterns to determine risk. Every on-time payment strengthens the pattern. Every missed payment weakens it. Over time, these patterns become predictive. And predictive behavior determines opportunity.

Understanding this changes how you see credit. It stops being something abstract and becomes something measurable. It becomes a record of behavior, not a judgment of character. That distinction is important, especially for anyone working to separate their past from their future.

But credit is more than borrowing money.

Credit is **trust**.

Credit is your **facecard**.

If you were a hustler on the streets, you know a lil something about that. Jackboyz facecard be on the floor because street niggas know they have no intentions on paying anything back. As a matter of fact, not only would the plug not serve them if they were on game about what type of time they were on, they would probably act like they wasn't holding because they don't even want this non-trustworthy individual to know they had anything worth stickin' them up for. Their street credit gets them denied every time. So, if that's their illegitimate credit, the concept that I'm trying to get you to grasp in this book is legal credit, the score connected to your Social Security number that lets creditors know if you handle your business.

Every time a lender extends credit to you, they're betting that you'll keep your word. Every time you pay on time — or don't — that trust is recorded. Over time, those records form your **credit history**, which becomes your financial reputation.

Whether you want housing, a job, utilities, transportation, or the ability to start over clean after release, your credit history plays a role.

CREDIT AS FINANCIAL TRUSTWORTHINESS

At its core, credit answers one question:

Can you be trusted to handle financial responsibility?

Landlords, lenders, employers, and utility companies all use credit data to help answer that question. They don't know you personally. They don't know your story. They rely on what your credit history shows.

That history is built through patterns.

Credit scoring systems are not reacting to one isolated decision.

They are analyzing repeated behavior over time. One mistake does not automatically define your credit profile, but repeated behavior does. Lenders are not measuring what you intended to do — they are measuring what your record consistently shows.

The system is built to evaluate patterns. Every financial action contributes to a larger track record that determines how much risk you represent. Those patterns are shaped by everyday decisions such as:

- Borrowing money
- Making payments on time (or late)
- Carrying balances
- Closing or defaulting on accounts

Individually, each action may seem small. But collectively, they form a predictable trend. And in the world of credit, trends carry more weight than explanations. Your financial history is judged by what you repeatedly do, not what you meant to do.

CREDIT HISTORY AND CREDIT REPORTS

Your **credit history** is the full record of how you've handled credit over time. That history is stored in a **credit report**, which is maintained by credit bureaus.

Each section in a credit report serves a different purpose in evaluating risk. Some items verify your identity and confirm you are who you claim to be. Others show how consistently you have handled financial obligations. Together, they create a detailed profile that lenders review before approving housing, utilities, loans, or employment where credit checks are involved.

Understanding what appears on your report helps you read it with intention instead of confusion. It also prepares you to recognize errors, outdated information, or signs of fraud later in this book. Your credit report includes:

- Personal identifying information
- Credit accounts (open and closed)

- Payment history
- Amounts owed
- Collections and bankruptcies
- Credit inquiries

This is what lenders and others review when deciding whether to approve you, deny you, or charge you higher costs.

✓ Previously Learned

Credit reports track **financial behavior only**. Arrests, convictions, and incarceration **never appear** on a credit report.

CREDIT SCORES: YOUR FINANCIAL SNAPSHOT

A **credit score** is a three-digit number (typically between 300 and 850) that summarizes your credit report. Instead of reading every detail, lenders use this number to quickly judge risk.

Higher scores mean:

- More approvals
- Lower deposits
- Lower interest rates

Lower scores mean:

- Denials
- Higher costs
- Fewer options

Credit scores are not opinions. They are math — based entirely on what appears in your credit report.

HOW CREDIT SCORES ARE CALCULATED

Most lenders use the **FICO score**, which is calculated using five main factors:

Payment History (35%)

- Do you pay bills on time?
- Late payments, collections, charge-offs, and bankruptcies damage this area. Consistent on-time payments strengthen it.

Amounts Owed / Credit Utilization (30%)

- How much of your available credit are you using?
- High balances compared to limits hurt your score. Lower balances help.
- **General rule:** Keep usage under 30%.
- **Best practice:** 1–10% if possible.

Length of Credit History (15%)

- How long have your accounts existed?
- Older accounts help. Closing long-standing accounts can hurt.

Credit Mix (10%)

- Do you handle different types of credit?
- A mix of revolving (credit cards) and installment (loans) is ideal.

New Credit (10%)

- How often do you apply for new credit?
- Too many applications in a short time can lower your score temporarily.

✓ Previously Learned

Your income, job, criminal record, and incarceration status are **not factors** in your credit score.

TYPES OF CREDIT

Understanding credit types helps you read your report and build strategically.

Installment Credit

Loans with fixed payments over time. Examples:

- Auto loans
- Student loans
- Personal loans

Revolving Credit

Credit with a limit that you can reuse. Examples:

- Credit cards
- Lines of credit

Open Credit

Balances must be paid in full each cycle. Examples:

- Some charge cards
- Certain utility accounts

A healthy credit profile usually includes **more than one type**.

CREDIT BUREAUS: WHO TRACKS YOUR CREDIT

There are three major credit bureaus in the United States:

- Experian
- Equifax
- TransUnion

Each bureau maintains its **own version** of your credit report. Not all creditors report to all bureaus, which is why reports can differ.

Now, let's bring this to the streets again right fast. Hustlers talk. So, let's look at the three credit bureaus as the major plugs 'round yo way. Every trap you hit, you wonder why you can't get no dope, and the reason being is because all three of them have the understanding that you some bullshit. They keep their ears to the street, and the consensus is always the same: you take too long to pay, don't pay at all, remix the packs, or just straight up run off.

In essence… you're a fuckin' *turd.*

What's a *turd,* you ask?

Well, let's explore this, shall we…

Turd - an individual who demonstrates a consistent lack of ambition, poor decision-making, and a disregard for personal responsibility, resulting in minimal motivation, low aspiration, and diminished social credibility. Such a person exhibits disengagement from purposeful living, rejects self-improvement, and fails to contribute positively to their own development or the respect of others. A "turd" is not defined by circumstance but by an unwillingness to strive for respect, progress, or meaningful achievement.

Nah, I'm bullshittin'. Lol. I actually just made that up to make it sound extra sophisticated. A turd is doo-doo. A piece of shit. And that's exactly how lenders and creditors will look at you if you pop out on the scene doing bad business. Even worse, they'll treat you like shit too.

I still like that definition, though. It's figuratively accurate ✓✓✓.

In this book, the word turd does not refer to an insult, but to a mindset. It is not a description of where a person comes from, but of the choices they repeatedly make and the standards they refuse to uphold.

A good name is worth more than silver and gold. Every real street nigga knows this. It makes it easier to do business and work yo move. You don't want people scared to serve you or shop with you. That type of stuff slows the money up. If you had a good name in the streets, this is very much the same. If you was some bullshit out there, don't bring that mentality into your legitimate dealings too. Remember how difficult being known for bullshit was. Trying to convince everybody you did business with that you wasn't on that this time or that your dope wasn't flex and that it actually weighed what you said it did. This is a fresh start in a whole different ball game, one that's attached to your Social Security number. Ain't no outrunning that.

Million-dollar tip: stand on business.

✓ Previously Learned

Fixing your credit with one bureau does **not** automatically fix it with the others.

CREDIT REPORTS VS. CREDIT SCORES (CLEAR DIFFERENCE)

Credit Report	Credit Score
Detailed History	Three-Digit Summary
Shows All Accounts	Measures Risk
Used For Disputes	Used For Decisions
Free By Mail	Sometimes Costs

Your **report feeds your score**.
Fix the report and the score follows.

WHO USES YOUR CREDIT INFORMATION

Credit reports and scores are used by:

- Lenders and banks
- Landlords and property managers
- Utility companies
- Employers (certain positions)
- Insurance companies
- Government agencies
- Collection agencies

Most importantly — you should use it **yourself** to protect and prepare your future. You ain't do all this time holdin' it down in prison to get out and be a turd.

WHY CREDIT MATTERS NOW — NOT LATER

Credit does not pause because you're locked up. It's layin' on you to get out like a lifelong opp. Old debts don't disappear. Errors don't fix themselves, and identity theft can happen without you knowing. This is your leverage we're talking about here. That's not something you want to leave to chance.

Knowledge shifts your timeline. Instead of waiting until release to discover problems, you gain the advantage of preparation while time is still on your side. Early awareness transforms credit from something reactive into something strategic. When you understand how it works, you stop guessing and start making deliberate decisions.

Preparation does not require freedom; it requires information. And information creates leverage.

Understanding credit now allows you to:

- Catch mistakes early

- Protect your identity
- Prepare for release
- Avoid starting from behind

✓ Previously Learned
Time alone does **not** fix credit. Action does.

Why This Matters

Understanding credit is not about becoming an expert in finance. It is about protecting your future choices. Credit affects where you can live, how much you pay for transportation, and whether opportunities are available to you after release. Without understanding how credit works, decisions are made blindly and mistakes repeat themselves.

For incarcerated individuals, credit knowledge restores a sense of control. Even while physically restricted, learning how credit works allows you to prepare for independence and stability. Knowledge becomes a form of preparation, and preparation becomes power.

Reflection Questions

1. What did I learn about credit that I did not know before?
2. How has my past behavior affected my credit today?
3. Why does credit matter for my future goals?
4. What mistakes do I want to avoid repeating?
5. What does responsible credit use look like for me?

Action Steps

- Write down what you believe your current credit situation is
- Identify one habit you need to change moving forward
- Commit to learning more before taking any action
- Begin keeping a credit notebook or folder

CHAPTER 1 TAKEAWAYS

- Credit is financial trust.
- Credit reports track history; scores summarize risk.
- Criminal records are never part of credit files.
- You can understand and prepare from prison.
- Knowledge now saves years later.
- Don't be a turd.

Chapter 2 will show you how to **access your credit reports from prison** and identify exactly where you stand.

Assessing Your Current Credit Status from Prison

"Even from behind bars, it's essential to understand your credit and finances; knowledge is power, and it can help break the cycle of poverty and incarceration."

- Marsha Jones

WHY ASSESSING YOUR CREDIT COMES FIRST

Before you can fix, build, or protect your credit, you need to know **exactly where you stand**. Guessing won't help you. Hope won't help you. Only facts will.

Most people avoid checking their credit because they fear what they might find. But uncertainty is more dangerous than bad information. If your credit is strong, confirmation builds confidence. If your credit is damaged, awareness creates a starting point. Either outcome gives you control.

Assessment is not about shame. It is about strategy. You can't build a plan around assumptions. You build it around facts. The sooner those facts are clear, the sooner improvement begins.

Your credit report is the starting point. It tells you:

- What accounts exist in your name
- What debts are unpaid
- Whether errors or fraud occurred while you were locked up
- What lenders will see when you're released

This is the rundown the three major plugs have on you as you move about these legit streets. Without this information, every move you make is blind.

YOUR LEGAL RIGHT TO ACCESS CREDIT REPORTS

Before you fix anything, you need to understand something important: access to your credit report is not a privilege; it's a legal right. The credit reporting system was not designed to operate in secrecy. Federal law requires transparency because inaccurate information can affect housing, employment, loans, and opportunity. That protection applies to every consumer, including prisoners.

Your physical location does not cancel your consumer rights. Being behind the wall does not suspend the Fair Credit Reporting Act. Credit bureaus are required to provide you access to the financial information they are reporting under your name. If decisions can be made about you using that data, you have the right to see it.

This matters because knowledge eliminates guesswork. Instead of assuming your credit is damaged or assuming it's fine, you replace uncertainty with documented facts. From prison, that clarity is power.

Under federal law, you are entitled to the following:

- **One free credit report every 12 months** from each bureau
- Additional free reports if:
    - You were denied credit, housing, or employment in the last 60 days
    - You are a victim of identity theft

- You are unemployed and seeking work

✓ Previously Learned

Credit bureaus do not know you are incarcerated. Your credit file continues to exist and update unless you intervene.

HOW TO ORDER YOUR CREDIT REPORT FROM PRISON

Because internet and phone access is limited, **mail is your primary method**.

Step 1: Gather Required Information

Accuracy at this stage prevents delays later. Credit bureaus verify identity carefully before releasing reports, especially when requests come by mail. Incomplete information, missing prior addresses, or mismatched names can cause your request to be rejected or stalled. That means more waiting, more letters, and more frustration.

Preparation is what keeps this process smooth. Even from prison, organization matters. The more precise your information is, the faster your report can be processed and returned. Taking a few extra minutes to gather everything correctly reduces the risk of starting over.

To avoid unnecessary delays, prepare the following:

- Full legal name (include aliases if used)
- Date of birth
- Social Security number
- Current prison address (include inmate number if required)
- Previous addresses from the last 2–5 years (if possible)

Step 2: Proof of Identity

Credit bureaus can't release your report without verifying that you are who you claim to be. This requirement protects you from someone else requesting your credit file fraudulently. While that protection is necessary, it also means your request will be denied if proper identification is not included.

Many requests from incarcerated individuals are delayed simply because proof of identity was incomplete, unclear, or missing. Mailing original documents is never required — and never recommended. Originals can be lost, misrouted, or damaged in transit, especially within correctional mail systems.

Your goal is to provide enough documentation to confirm your identity without creating unnecessary risk. Clear copies and complete information reduce rejection and shorten processing time.

To verify your identity, include copies of the following:

- Prison ID or DOC identification sheet
- Social Security card (if available)
- Any official mail showing your prison address

Step 3: Write a Simple Request Letter

Use clear, direct language.

Sample Letter:

Dear [Credit Bureau],

I am requesting a copy of my credit report under the Fair Credit Reporting Act. I am currently incarcerated. Please mail my report to the address listed below.

Thank you for your assistance.

Step 4: Mail Your Request

You may write to each bureau individually **or** use the centralized service.

Centralized Address (All Three Bureaus):

Annual Credit Report Request Service
P.O. Box 105281
Atlanta, GA 30348-5281

Step 5: Track and Keep Copies

- Keep copies of everything you send
- Use certified mail if possible
- Expect a response within **2–4 weeks** (sometimes longer due to prison mail delays)

WHAT TO DO IF YOUR REPORT DOESN'T ARRIVE

Silence does not mean denial. Mail delays are common, especially within correctional facilities. Processing times at credit bureaus can vary, and when prison mailrooms are involved, timelines can stretch beyond what is typical on the outside.

It is important not to interpret a delay as rejection or failure. Bureaucratic systems move slowly, but they do move. The key here is controlled persistence, not frustration. One unanswered request does not mean you can't access your report. It simply means you must follow up.

The difference between people who gain control of their credit and those who stay stuck is often persistence. If your report does not arrive within a reasonable timeframe, take the next step calmly and methodically.

If 30 days pass with no response:

- Send a follow-up letter
- Include a copy of your original request
- Check with your facility's mailroom or reentry office

Persistence matters here.

UNDERSTANDING YOUR CREDIT REPORT

Once your report arrives, don't rush. Read it **line by line**.

Your credit report is divided into key sections.

1. Personal Information

Check for:

- Misspelled names
- Incorrect birth dates
- Addresses you don't recognize

Errors here can signal identity mix-ups or fraud.

2. Credit Accounts (Tradelines)

This section lists:

- Credit cards
- Loans
- Retail accounts

Each account shows:

- Open/close dates
- Balance
- Payment history
- Account status

This is where lenders judge your reliability.

3. Collections

These are accounts sent to collection agencies due to nonpayment.

Collections **seriously damage** credit and must be reviewed carefully for accuracy.

4. Public Records

Includes:

- Bankruptcies
- Certain financial judgments

✓ Previously Learned

Criminal charges, convictions, and prison sentences never appear in this section.

5. Credit Inquiries

- **Hard inquiries:** Applications for credit (affect score temporarily)
- **Soft inquiries:** Monitoring or pre-screening (no impact)

Unrecognized hard inquiries can indicate fraud.

6. Payment History

This shows month-by-month performance:

- On-time
- 30 / 60 / 90+ days late

Payment history is the **most influential factor** in your credit score.

SIGNS OF IDENTITY THEFT OR INACCURACIES

Because incarcerated people are at higher risk, watch closely for:

- Accounts you never opened
- Loans or cards from unfamiliar lenders

- Addresses you've never lived at
- Sudden balances or defaults you don't recognize
- Duplicate or outdated accounts

Not all errors are fraud, but **all errors must be challenged**.

WHAT TO DO IF YOU FIND ERRORS OR FRAUD

Step 1: Document Everything

- Highlight incorrect items
- Write down account names, numbers, and dates

Step 2: Dispute in Writing

Send disputes to **each bureau reporting the error**.
Include:

- Clear explanation
- Supporting documents
- Copy of your ID

Step 3: Follow Up

Bureaus have **30 days** to investigate. If unresolved, dispute again.

✓ Previously Learned

Fixing errors on your credit report is one of the fastest ways to improve your score.

IDENTIFYING YOUR STARTING POINT

After reviewing your report, you'll fall into **one of three categories**:

1. No Credit

- No accounts
- No score

This is not bad. It means you can start clean.

2. Thin Credit File

- One or two accounts
- Limited history

This can be strengthened with careful additions.

3. Damaged Credit

- Late payments
- Collections
- Charge-offs

This requires repair before rebuilding.

Knowing your category determines your strategy.

If You Already Have Good Credit

If you're reading this and your credit is already in good standing, no late payments, solid score, positive accounts, etc., then you're in a powerful position.

But understand this: good credit is not the finish line. It's leverage.

This book will help you:

- Increase your score even further by optimizing utilization, payment timing, and account mix
- Strengthen your profile so lenders see you as low-risk and high-value
- Build intelligently by adding the right accounts instead of unnecessary ones
- Avoid common mistakes that cause people to fall from good credit into damaged credit

Most importantly, it will give you a complete understanding of how credit actually works, so you're not just using it, you're controlling it.

A Final Word

I wrote this book with a specific purpose in mind. This is for people who feel like they're starting from behind. People in prison with little to no understanding of credit, trying to figure it out like I was. Striving to rebuild their life financially from limited access, limited information, and limited opportunity. This book is for the ones starting with nothing. Its for the ones trying to fix what's already broken. But if you're already ahead, this book is still for you. Use it as a framework. Use it as a blueprint.

Use it to make sure you never have to start over again.

Why This Matters

You can't improve what you can't see. Knowing what is on your credit report is the starting point for every other step in this book. Many people leave prison unaware that their credit has been damaged or misused during incarceration. That surprise can create setbacks at the exact moment when stability is needed most.

This chapter matters because awareness prevents shock. When you know your credit situation in advance, you can plan instead of panic. Preparation reduces stress and increases confidence during reentry.

Reflection Questions

1. Do I currently know what is on my credit report?
2. Who can help me access my credit information?
3. What fears do I have about checking my credit?
4. What would I do if I found errors?
5. How would knowing my credit help me plan?

Action Steps

- Decide how you will request your credit reports
- Identify a trusted outside helper if needed
- Create a tracking log for credit requests
- Prepare to review reports carefully when received

CHAPTER 2 TAKEAWAYS

- You have the legal right to your credit report.
- Mail requests work — even from prison.
- Your report tells the full financial story.
- Errors and fraud must be disputed immediately.
- Your starting point matters more than your past.

Chapter 3 will focus on **protecting your credit and disputing errors effectively while incarcerated**.

Protecting Your Credit and Disputing Errors from Prison

"What you don't check, you can't correct."

- Anonymous

WHY CREDIT PROTECTION MATTERS WHILE YOU'RE INCARCERATED

Being incarcerated does **not** protect your credit. In fact, it can make you more vulnerable. Being locked up limits physical freedom, but it does not pause financial exposure. Reduced access to your own information increases vulnerability. Systems continue to operate. Data continues to move. Accounts can be opened, balances can change, and errors can occur without your knowledge. That delay between activity and discovery is what makes credit protection critical during your time behind the wall.

Protection is not paranoia. It is preparation. The goal is not to live in fear of fraud, but to reduce the likelihood of surprise damage at the exact moment stability matters most.

When you're locked up:

- You aren't monitoring your accounts daily.
- Mail delays are common.
- Identity thieves assume you won't notice problems quickly.

That's why protecting your credit is just as important as building it. If you don't actively check and defend your credit file, mistakes and fraud can quietly damage your future.

COMMON CREDIT RISKS FOR INCARCERATED PEOPLE

While many readers may assume identity theft only happens to people actively using credit and financial services, incarcerated individuals are targeted precisely because they are out of sight and unable to monitor their financial identities. A National Consumer Law Center (NCLC) article reported that identity thieves have long exploited the reality that people in prison rarely have real-time access to their credit reports or financial accounts, making mistakes or fraudulent accounts slow to surface and even slower to resolve. In some documented cases, fraudsters have even used prisoners' personal identifying information — such as names, Social Security numbers, and birthdates — to open federal student loans, bank accounts, and other financial products, while the victims remain locked away and unaware.

Experts point out that incarcerated people are attractive targets because they can't easily monitor credit activity, challenge suspicious inquiries, or dispute unauthorized accounts in real time. In one reported incident, dozens of prisoners' identities were used to apply for more than $400,000 in federal student loans, all while those individuals were still serving long sentences and unable to check their own credit. Identity thieves don't need internet access to take advantage; they only need enough information to satisfy institutions' verification processes, and then they can build credit or rack up debt using someone else's name.

In addition to outside fraud rings, there have also been cases where insiders within the corrections system facilitated identity theft. In one historic example, there was an incident reported in Prison Legal News (PLN) where a juvenile correctional officer stole the personal information of nearly 50 current and former juvenile offenders then used that data to file fraudulent tax returns in the inmates' names — collecting refunds without the victims ever knowing their identities had been misused.

Crazy but true. Even crazier is the fact that these cases ain't isolated incidents or rare exceptions. They illustrate a broader reality: incarceration creates conditions that make identity theft easier and more profitable for scammers. Understanding these heightened vulnerabilities is essential because the risks faced while incarcerated ain't the same as those faced on the outside. The following points outline the specific ways incarceration increases exposure to identity theft and credit abuse:

- Identity theft using your Social Security number
- Accounts opened without your knowledge
- Old debts misreported or duplicated
- Late payments reported during incarceration
- Collections for bills you never received

These issues don't fix themselves. If left alone, they follow you into release. That's what you don't want. So, why not focus on these things now while you have nothing but time? So many of us are behind the wall doing dead time… don't be a turd.

✓ Previously Learned

Credit bureaus do not know your circumstances. They only report what creditors send them.

MONITORING YOUR CREDIT FROM PRISON

Monitoring your credit while incarcerated requires a different mindset than monitoring it on the outside. You do not have real-time alerts, mobile apps, or immediate access to financial statements. That limitation makes structure even more important. Without a system, months or even years can pass before errors or unauthorized activity are discovered.

Monitoring is not about expecting something to go wrong. It is about shortening the gap between activity and awareness. The longer negative information sits undiscovered, the harder it can become to correct. Consistent review creates control. Even if nothing changes, confirmation is valuable.

Because access is limited, monitoring from prison must be intentional and periodic. You can't check daily, so you build a schedule and stick to it.

You should:

- Request your credit reports at least once per year
- Space requests across bureaus if possible
- Review every report line by line
- Keep copies of all correspondence

If you have a trusted outside contact, they can help monitor alerts or receive correspondence — but only with your written authorization.

WHAT COUNTS AS A CREDIT ERROR?

Not every negative item on your credit report is an error. Some entries reflect real past behavior. The goal is not to dispute accurate information simply because it is unfavorable. The goal is to identify information that is inaccurate, outdated, incomplete, or unverifiable.

A credit error is any information that does not correctly represent your financial history. Even small inaccuracies can affect your score, your approval odds, or the terms you are offered. Lenders rely on data — not explanations. If the data is wrong, your profile is wrong.

Understanding what qualifies as an error prevents wasted disputes and increases your credibility when you do challenge something. You ain't trying to erase history. You are trying to ensure it is reported correctly.

The following situations qualify as credit errors:

- Accounts you never opened
- Incorrect balances
- Late payments reported incorrectly
- Duplicate collections
- Accounts showing open when they are closed
- Debts past the legal reporting time

Errors are more common than most people think.

YOUR LEGAL RIGHT TO DISPUTE ERRORS

Before the Fair Credit Reporting Act existed, credit reporting operated with almost no accountability. Credit bureaus collected and shared financial information about people, but consumers had little to no ability to see what was being reported, challenge mistakes, or correct false information. Errors could follow someone for years — denials for housing, employment, or credit — with no meaningful way to fight back.

As credit became more central to everyday life, these errors caused real harm. People were denied loans, apartments, and jobs based on inaccurate or outdated information, often without ever knowing why. There were widespread complaints about mixed files, incorrect balances, debts that didn't belong to the consumer, and information that should have been removed but wasn't. The system favored convenience for lenders over fairness for individuals.

In response to growing public pressure, the United States Congress passed the Fair Credit Reporting Act in 1970. The purpose of the law was simple but powerful: to force accuracy, fairness, and accountability into the credit reporting system. For the first time, consumers were given the legal right to access their credit information, dispute errors, and require credit bureaus and creditors to investigate and correct inaccurate reporting.

Under the **Fair Credit Reporting Act (FCRA)**, you have the right to challenge inaccurate information.

Once you dispute:

- The credit bureau must investigate.
- Creditors must verify the information.
- Unverified items must be corrected or removed.

This applies even while incarcerated.

✓ Previously Learned

Fixing errors on your credit report is one of the fastest ways to improve your credit score.

HOW TO DISPUTE CREDIT ERRORS BY MAIL (STEP-BY-STEP)

Because you're in prison, **written disputes are the safest and strongest method**.

Step 1: Identify the Error Clearly

Write down:

- Creditor name
- Account number (partial if shown)
- Exact reason it's incorrect

Be specific. Vague disputes get ignored.

Step 2: Write a Dispute Letter

Each bureau must be disputed **separately**.
What to include:

- Your full legal name
- Date of birth

- Social Security number
- Prison address
- Clear explanation of the error
- Copies of supporting documents

Sample language:

I am disputing the accuracy of the following account. I do not recognize this account / the information reported is incorrect. Please investigate and correct or remove this item under the Fair Credit Reporting Act.

Step 3: Attach Supporting Documentation

Only include **copies**, never originals:

- Prison ID
- Court paperwork (if relevant)
- Account statements
- Prior correspondence

If you have no documents, state that clearly.

Step 4: Mail and Track Everything

- Send disputes to each bureau reporting the error
- Use certified mail if possible
- Keep copies of all letters
- Write down dates sent

Credit bureaus have **30 days** to respond.

WHAT HAPPENS AFTER YOU DISPUTE

After investigation, the bureau will:

- Correct the error
- Remove the item
- Or verify it as accurate

If verified and you still disagree:

- Dispute again
- Request the method of verification
- Dispute directly with the creditor

Persistence matters.

FRAUD ALERTS AND CREDIT FREEZES (OPTIONAL PROTECTION)

If you believe your identity has been compromised, you may request:

Fraud Alert

- Adds a warning to your credit file
- Lasts one year (renewable)
- Makes lenders verify identity before approval

Credit Freeze

- Blocks new credit from being opened
- Strongest protection
- Requires written request by mail

These tools can be used while incarcerated.

✓ Previously Learned

Credit protection is about preventing future damage — not just fixing past mistakes.

WORKING WITH OUTSIDE CONTACTS SAFELY

Prison limits access, which means you may need help from someone on the outside. Assistance can be valuable, but it must be structured. Trust without boundaries creates vulnerability, not protection.

Emotional closeness does not replace financial oversight. Even well-intentioned friends or family members can make mistakes if expectations are unclear. In some cases, relationships change, communication breaks down, or personal conflicts spill into financial matters. When credit is involved, those consequences follow you — not them.

If someone is assisting you with monitoring, correspondence, or account management, define the role clearly. Help should increase control, not reduce it. Structure protects both your credit and your relationships.

If someone is helping you:

- Use written authorization
- Never share your SSN casually
- Set clear limits on what they can do
- Review everything they touch

Help is useful — but trust must be controlled.

Why This Matters

Errors on your credit report are not just paperwork problems. They can block housing, raise interest rates, and limit employment opportunities. For incarcerated individuals, mistakes are harder to detect and slower to correct, which makes them more dangerous.

Disputing errors is not complaining; it is protecting your record. This chapter matters because it teaches you to defend yourself in a system that does not automatically correct its own mistakes. Your future depends on accuracy.

Reflection Questions

1. Why is it important to correct errors instead of ignoring them?
2. What risks do incarcerated people face that others may not?
3. How could identity theft affect my future?
4. What rights do I have under the law?
5. What would I do first if fraud appeared on my report?

Action Steps

- Write a plan for how you would dispute an error
- Gather any documents you may need
- Create a simple recordkeeping system
- Stay alert for signs of misuse

CHAPTER 3 TAKEAWAYS

- Incarceration increases credit risk.
- Errors and fraud are common — but fixable.
- You have legal dispute rights.
- Written disputes work from prison.
- Protection now prevents setbacks later.

Chapter 4 will focus on **building positive credit activity**, even with limited access and income.

Protecting Yourself from Identity Theft While Incarcerated

"Your credit report is your financial fingerprint. Protect it like your identity depends on it — because it does."

- Him 500

WHY IDENTITY THEFT IS A BIGGER RISK IN PRISON: THE FOLLOW UP

Like I said in Chapter 3, incarceration doesn't freeze your identity — it **exposes it**.

When you're locked up:

- You aren't watching your credit daily.
- Your personal information exists in multiple systems.
- Mail delays slow your response time.
- Criminals assume you won't notice fraud quickly.

That combination makes incarcerated people **prime targets** for identity theft. Most victims don't discover the damage until release… when housing, jobs, or utilities are denied.

Identity theft thrives where oversight is weakest. When individuals can't monitor their accounts in real time, fraud becomes easier to execute and harder to detect. The longer unauthorized activity goes unnoticed, the more complicated the resolution process becomes. That delay is costly, especially when preparing for reentry.

Prevention requires understanding that identity protection is not optional maintenance. It is structural defense. A single fraudulent account can undo months of careful preparation. That risk justifies vigilance.

Let's be real… the last thing you need is a bad facecard. How you gone lose in the streets and on the straight and narrow? At some point, it's like goddamn. Pick a struggle. This chapter is about making sure that **doesn't happen to you**.

WHAT IDENTITY THEFT LOOKS LIKE ON A CREDIT REPORT

Identity theft rarely begins with something obvious. It does not always show up as a massive loan or a maxed-out credit card overnight. In many cases, it starts with small activity designed to test whether anyone is watching. A single unfamiliar inquiry. A new address attached to your file. A minor account opened quietly.

Because incarcerated individuals do not have daily access to their financial records, small warning signs can go unnoticed for extended periods. What might seem insignificant at first can become serious damage if ignored. The earlier you recognize irregular activity, the easier it is to contain.

The key is not panic; it's pattern recognition. Your credit report tells a story. If part of that story doesn't match your real financial history, it deserves attention.

Watch for:

- Credit cards or loans you never applied for
- Utility or phone accounts opened without your knowledge

- Addresses you've never lived at
- Hard inquiries you don't recognize
- Collections tied to unfamiliar accounts

✓ Previously Learned

Credit bureaus do not verify intent or circumstances. They report what creditors submit.

If it's wrong, **you must challenge it**.

WHY PRISONERS ARE SPECIFICALLY TARGETED

Identity thieves target incarcerated people because:

- Monitoring is infrequent
- Victims are harder to reach
- Delays benefit the criminal
- Many assume prisoners won't fight back

This isn't paranoia — it's documented reality.

THE FIRST LINE OF DEFENSE: MONITORING

You can't stop what you don't see.

From prison, monitoring means:

- Ordering credit reports regularly
- Spacing requests across bureaus
- Reviewing every line, every time
- Keeping a written log of changes

If you have an outside contact helping you, they should **monitor; not control**.

CREDIT FREEZES: YOUR STRONGEST PROTECTION TOOL

A **credit freeze** blocks new credit from being opened in your name.

What it does:

- Prevents new accounts
- Stops most identity theft cold
- Does not affect existing accounts
- Is free by law

You can request a freeze **by mail** with each bureau.

✓ Previously Learned

A credit freeze prevents future damage — it does not fix existing errors.

Freezes are protection, not repair.

FRAUD ALERTS: EXTRA WARNING, NOT A LOCK

A **fraud alert** places a warning on your credit file telling lenders to verify identity.

Key points:

- Lasts one year (renewable)
- Easier to set than a freeze
- Still allows credit to be opened
- Less secure than a freeze

Fraud alerts are helpful, but **not foolproof**.

WHICH IS BETTER WHILE INCARCERATED?

If you don't expect to apply for credit soon, a freeze makes the most sense. While I was in the process of building my credit, I simply did a fraud alert because I knew I would be opening accounts. However, I did have my outside contact open a Smart Credit account.

Smart Credit is a credit monitoring and identity-tracking service designed to alert you when changes occur on your credit file. Instead of waiting months to discover fraud or errors, Smart Credit sends notifications when new accounts, inquiries, or personal information updates appear on your credit report.

Its purpose is not to prevent identity theft by itself, but to help you detect problems early so action can be taken quickly. For incarcerated individuals, this usually means an outside contact is responsible for reviewing alerts and reporting suspicious activity back to you.

Smart Credit functions as an early warning system that can support either a fraud alert or a credit freeze strategy, depending on your situation. This means Smart Credit should be viewed as a support tool, not a replacement for protection. I only made mention of it to share my experience. If this works for you, use it. If it doesn't sound ideal, disregard it.

With that said, for most incarcerated individuals, the answer is clear:

- Credit Freeze = best option
- Fraud Alert = backup layer

A credit freeze makes the most sense because:

- You are unlikely to apply for credit while incarcerated.
- It prevents criminals from opening accounts in your name.
- It removes the need for constant monitoring.
- It provides the strongest protection available.

A fraud alert may be more appropriate if:

- You plan to actively build credit
- You expect to open new accounts
- You need lenders to still access your file
- You have an outside helper assisting you

However, a fraud alert still allows credit to be opened, which creates risk.

PROTECTING YOUR PERSONAL INFORMATION

Identity theft rarely begins with sophisticated hacking. More often, it begins with casual access — information shared too freely, documents signed without clarity, or authority granted without limits. Incarceration creates distance, and distance increases reliance on others. That reliance must be structured.

Your personal information — your Social Security number, date of birth, full legal name, and identifying documents — is the key to your financial identity. Once released into the wrong hands, it can be used repeatedly without your awareness. Prevention is not about suspicion. It's about control.

Convenience is not protection. Allowing someone to "handle everything" may feel easier in the moment, but unrestricted access creates risk. Structure protects you. Clear boundaries protect your credit. Written limitations protect your future.

Be cautious with:

- Sharing Social Security numbers
- Signing blank forms
- Giving unrestricted power of attorney
- Letting others "handle everything"

If someone helps you, set limits.

USING OUTSIDE CONTACTS SAFELY

Help can be powerful… or dangerous.
Best practices:

- Use **written authorization only**
- Define exactly what they can do
- Review all documents they send or receive
- Never give full control without oversight

✓ Previously Learned

Trust without structure creates vulnerability.

IF IDENTITY THEFT IS CONFIRMED

If you discover fraud:

1. Dispute the account with all reporting bureaus
2. Dispute directly with the creditor
3. Request a credit freeze immediately
4. Document everything

Persistence is key. Fraud disputes often require follow-up.

HABITS THAT PROTECT YOU LONG-TERM

Identity protection isn't one move… it's a habit.
Build these habits now:

- Regular credit review
- Organized paperwork
- Written communication only
- Controlled access to your information

These habits will serve you **after release**, too.

. . .

Why This Matters

Identity theft does not announce itself. It does not ask permission. It does not care that you are incarcerated. It simply exploits gaps in oversight. When you are unable to monitor your credit in real time, those gaps widen.

For incarcerated individuals, identity theft is more than an inconvenience. It can delay housing approvals, complicate job opportunities, and create financial barriers at the exact moment stability is needed most. Discovering fraud after release forces you to fight paperwork battles while trying to rebuild your life.

This chapter matters because prevention is easier than repair. A credit freeze, structured monitoring, and controlled access to your personal information can prevent years of damage. Protection now eliminates chaos later. Your identity is tied to your future options. Guarding it is not optional; it's strategic.

Reflection Questions

1. Why am I vulnerable to identity theft right now?
2. Who currently has access to my personal information?
3. What protections have I put in place?
4. What would happen if my identity were stolen?
5. How can I reduce risk today?

Action Steps

- Decide between a credit freeze or fraud alert
- Identify who can help monitor your credit
- Limit who receives your personal information
- Store important documents safely

CHAPTER 4 TAKEAWAYS

- Incarceration increases identity theft risk.
- Monitoring is your first defense.
- Credit freezes offer the strongest protection.
- Fraud alerts add visibility, not security.
- Control over your data is non-negotiable.

Chapter 5 will focus on **building positive credit activity safely**, even with limited income and restricted access.

Building Credit from Prison — Small Actions, Real Progress

"Even from where you sit, you can build a future that stands — starting with small, consistent credit moves."

- Elijah R. Freeman

THE TRUTH ABOUT BUILDING CREDIT FROM PRISON

Let's be clear from the start: building credit from prison is **possible**, but it is not fast, flashy, or risky. There are no hacks, loopholes, or shortcuts that work safely from behind the wall.

What makes credit building from prison different is not the rules of credit — those remain the same — but the limitations on access, income, and communication. That means every move must be intentional. The margin for error is smaller, and the consequences of careless decisions are heavier. This chapter focuses on precision, not speed.

What *does* work is **structure, patience, and discipline**.

This chapter focuses on **realistic, low-risk ways** to begin building positive credit activity while incarcerated — or to prepare your credit profile so that building can begin immediately upon release.

WHAT "BUILDING CREDIT" ACTUALLY MEANS

Many people confuse credit activity with credit strength. They assume that opening more accounts, increasing limits, or using credit frequently equals progress. That misunderstanding is one of the fastest ways to create damage instead of growth.

Building credit is not about volume. It is about behavior. Credit scoring models are designed to measure consistency, not excitement. They reward predictable repayment patterns over time. The system does not care how ambitious you feel — it responds to whether your payments are made as agreed and whether balances remain controlled.

From prison, this distinction matters even more. Your margin for error is smaller. Every decision must be deliberate. Building credit means adding positive data slowly and avoiding unnecessary risk. It is about strengthening your financial reputation, not testing its limits.

Building credit does not mean:

- Taking on large debt
- Opening multiple accounts
- Chasing high limits
- Letting others run wild with your information

Building credit means:

- Adding **verified positive payment history**
- Keeping balances **low and controlled**
- Creating a **pattern of responsibility**
- Avoiding new damage while progress is made

✓ Previously Learned

Credit scores improve when positive activity is added — not just when negatives are removed.

Being added as an authorized user to one of my people's accounts was the first step for me on my credit journey. At the time, I wasn't even aware that that was something I could do. It's one of the safest credit-building options for an inmate if the person is reliable. I repeat, only if that person is reliable. Not a pen pal you met that you think you finessing because you call her your wife. Don't get slimed out tryna be cute. This is your future we talkin' bout here.

THE SAFEST CREDIT-BUILDING OPTIONS WHILE INCARCERATED

Because access is limited, your options must be **controlled and intentional**.

1. Authorized User Accounts (Used Correctly)

Being added as an authorized user on a **trusted person's** credit card can help your credit if done properly.

What works:

- The primary cardholder has good payment history.
- The balance stays low (under 30%, ideally under 10%).
- Payments are always on time.

What does NOT work:

- Maxed-out cards
- Missed payments
- Untrustworthy cardholders

You do **not** need physical access to the card for this to help your credit.

2. Preparing for Secured Credit After Release

If building credit while incarcerated is limited, **preparing** to build is still progress.

Use this time to:

- Clean errors from your credit report
- Resolve identity theft issues
- Organize documents
- Identify banks or credit unions that offer secured cards

This allows you to act immediately once released instead of losing months getting organized.

✓ Previously Learned

Credit repair clears the path. Credit building moves you forward.

CREDIT BUILDER LOANS: WHEN AND WHY THEY WORK

Credit builder loans are small loans where:

- Payments are reported to credit bureaus
- The money is released after payments are completed

These loans are best used:

- Through credit unions or community banks
- With small monthly payments
- Only when income is stable

They are **not ideal** if payments can't be guaranteed.

THE IMPORTANCE OF ON-TIME PAYMENTS (ABOVE ALL ELSE)

Nothing matters more than payment history. Nothing. Let that sink in.

One missed payment can:

- Undo months of progress
- Drop your score significantly
- Create new negative marks

If you can't guarantee payment: **Do not open the account yet.** Patience protects your progress.

KEEPING BALANCES LOW AND BEHAVIOR BORING

Credit does not reward flashiness. It rewards predictability. High balances, rapid spending, and frequent applications signal instability to scoring models, even if payments are made on time. The goal is not to look active — it is to look controlled.

Low balances protect your utilization ratio and create a buffer against mistakes. When balances remain small compared to available limits, your profile reflects discipline. Large balances, even if manageable, introduce risk. From a scoring perspective, risk is penalized.

"Boring" behavior in credit means resisting unnecessary movement. It means avoiding the urge to constantly adjust, apply, or increase limits. Stability over time builds confidence in your profile. Consistency becomes your advantage.

Best practices:

- Use little credit
- Pay balances down quickly
- Avoid unnecessary applications
- Let accounts age

✓ Previously Learned

The system rewards consistency, not creativity.

USING OUTSIDE CONTACTS WITHOUT LOSING CONTROL

Help can accelerate progress — **or destroy it**.

If someone is assisting you:

- Use written instructions
- Set strict limits
- Require updates and transparency
- Never hand over full control

You are building **your** credit, not outsourcing responsibility.

COMMON CREDIT-BUILDING MISTAKES TO AVOID

Most credit damage does not come from a lack of knowledge. It comes from impatience. When progress feels slow, the temptation to "speed things up" increases. That is where mistakes happen.

Building credit from prison — or after release — requires resisting the urge to overcorrect. Opening multiple accounts too quickly, testing limits, or chasing higher scores prematurely can create instability. Scoring systems are designed to detect sudden shifts in behavior. Rapid changes often look risky, even if intentions are good.

Another common mistake is emotional decision-making. Applying for credit because you feel behind, pressured, or eager to prove progress almost always leads to unnecessary risk. Discipline means moving according to plan — not according to mood.

Avoid:

- Opening too many accounts
- Letting others "experiment" with your credit

- Chasing fast results
- Ignoring statements or notices
- Applying for credit out of emotion

Progress is slow by design — and that's a good thing.

WHAT PROGRESS LOOKS LIKE (REALISTICALLY)

Credit improvement rarely feels dramatic. There is no single moment where everything changes overnight. Instead, progress appears quietly — through stability, small increases, and the absence of new damage. That quiet improvement is not weakness. It is strength.

Many people expect visible leaps: large score jumps, instant approvals, or rapid limit increases. When those things do not happen immediately, they assume nothing is working. In reality, slow progress is often the healthiest type of progress. It signals that your financial behavior is becoming predictable and reliable.

The key is recognizing growth even when it feels subtle. Stability is progress. Discipline is progress. The removal of risk is progress. When you shift your expectations from "fast" to "consistent", your mindset aligns with how credit actually works.

Progress may look like:

- One positive account added
- No new negative items
- Old errors removed
- Scores improving gradually
- Better options becoming available

That is **success**, even if it feels quiet.

BUILDING HABITS THAT LAST BEYOND RELEASE

What you practice now becomes automatic later.

Build habits of:

- Reviewing credit reports regularly
- Keeping records organized
- Paying attention to details
- Acting with intention

These habits matter more than any single account.

Why This Matters

Building credit from prison is not about speed. It is about foundation. Small, controlled actions create a pattern of responsibility that follows you long after release.

Many people come home and try to move fast — opening multiple accounts, chasing high limits, or reacting emotionally to past financial struggles. That approach often recreates the same instability they are trying to escape. Slow, intentional progress prevents that cycle.

This chapter matters because disciplined credit building changes your trajectory. A single positive account, handled correctly, is more powerful than multiple risky ones. When you understand that consistency outweighs volume, you stop chasing credit and start managing it. That shift builds leverage, and leverage creates options.

Reflection Questions

1. What habits protect my identity long-term?
2. How consistent have I been with monitoring?
3. Where do I need better structure?
4. What risks come from disorganization?
5. How can I improve my system?

. . .

Action Steps

- Create a monthly monitoring schedule
- Update your logs and records
- Review your protection strategy
- Make adjustments if something is not working

CHAPTER 5 TAKEAWAYS

- Credit can be built from prison — safely and slowly.
- Authorized users and preparation matter.
- On-time payments outweigh everything else.
- Control beats speed.
- Discipline creates options.

Chapter 6 will focus on **using credit responsibly after release**, so progress continues instead of resets.

Maintaining and Growing Your Score While Incarcerated

"Success is not built on what you do occasionally, but on what you do consistently."

- Eric Thomas

WHY THIS CHAPTER MATTERS

At this point, you've already done important work. You understand what credit is, how to access your reports, how to correct errors, and how to protect yourself from fraud while incarcerated.

What many people do not realize is that credit damage often happens quietly — not through major mistakes but through small lapses, overlooked accounts, or passive neglect. Maintenance requires attention even when nothing seems urgent. This chapter shifts your focus from fixing problems to preventing them.

What comes next is just as important but less talked about.

This chapter is about **maintenance and slow growth**.

While incarcerated, your credit journey is not about aggressive moves or rapid gains. It's about **preserving what you have, preventing silent damage, and allowing time to work in your favor**.

Credit responds to behavior and time. Even while incarcerated, both still matter.

WHAT "MAINTAINING" YOUR CREDIT REALLY MEANS

Maintaining your credit is often misunderstood as passive behavior. Many people believe that if they ain't opening new accounts or using credit actively, nothing significant is happening. That assumption is inaccurate. Credit files continue to evolve over time, whether you are paying attention or not.

Maintenance is about preservation. It is about protecting the stability you have already built. While building credit focuses on adding positive activity, maintaining credit focuses on preventing erosion. Small shifts — account closures, rising balances, missed notices — can quietly weaken a profile that once looked strong.

Incarceration increases the importance of maintenance because access is limited. You can't react quickly to every change. That means your strategy must prioritize stability and prevention over expansion. Maintaining your credit is not inactivity. It is disciplined protection.

It means:

- Preventing unnecessary score drops
- Keeping positive accounts intact
- Avoiding actions that quietly cause harm
- Monitoring changes over time

Many people assume that if they ain't actively using credit, nothing is happening. That assumption is dangerous.

Credit files change even when you're not paying attention.

THE RISK OF INACTION

In credit, doing nothing is not neutral. It is often interpreted as instability. Many lenders automatically close accounts after long periods of inactivity. While that may seem harmless, closed accounts can reduce your available credit and weaken the structure of your profile.

Incarceration increases the likelihood of inactivity. If accounts are left untouched without a plan, creditors may close them to manage their own risk. When that happens, your total available credit decreases. Even if your balances remain the same, your utilization ratio can rise simply because your limits have dropped.

Inaction can also create stagnation. Without careful oversight, minor issues may go unnoticed. Over time, small unaddressed changes can quietly reduce your score. Stability requires awareness, not passivity.

Inaction can lead to:

- Accounts being closed due to inactivity
- Reduced available credit
- Higher utilization ratios caused by closures
- A stagnant or weakening credit profile

None of these involve fraud or errors. They happen quietly, often without notice.

✓ Previously Learned

Credit bureaus report what creditors send them, not what you intended to do.

If an account closes, the impact is real — regardless of why it happened.

PROTECTING THE AGE OF YOUR CREDIT

The **length of your credit history** is one of the most overlooked factors affecting your score.

Older accounts:

- Strengthen your credit profile
- Show stability
- Offset newer negative items

Closing old accounts — especially unnecessarily — can shorten your credit history and hurt your score.

While incarcerated:

- Avoid closing long-standing accounts unless absolutely necessary
- Think carefully before allowing others to close accounts "to clean things up"
- Understand that time itself is helping your credit age

Patience is not passive. It is strategic.

MANAGING UTILIZATION WITHOUT ACTIVE SPENDING

Credit utilization is based on **balances compared to available limits**.

Even if you are not actively using credit:

- Closed accounts can increase utilization
- Authorized user balances can affect your ratio
- Small balances can still have an impact

Monitoring utilization through periodic credit reports is essential.

If someone else controls an account you're attached to, their behavior affects your score — whether you spend or not.

AUTHORIZED USER STATUS: LONG-TERM DISCIPLINE

Authorized user accounts can help or hurt over time.

While incarcerated, authorized user status should be treated as a **maintenance tool**, not a shortcut.

Key rules:

- Stay attached only to accounts with consistent on-time payments
- Monitor balances regularly through reports
- Be willing to remove yourself if the account becomes risky
- Do not "set it and forget it"

Authorized user status requires ongoing oversight.

✓ Previously Learned

Help without structure creates risk.

HOW CREDIT CAN STILL GROW WHILE YOU'RE INCARCERATED

Credit growth during incarceration is **slow, but real.**

Scores can improve through:

- Aging accounts
- Lower utilization ratios
- Removal of negative items
- Long-term stability

This type of growth doesn't feel dramatic, but it is durable.

You ain't tryna "build fast".

You are creating a **strong foundation**.

MONITORING STRATEGY FOR LONG SENTENCES

Monitoring is different when incarceration is measured in years.

A realistic approach includes:

- Requesting reports on a consistent schedule
- Rotating bureaus when possible
- Comparing reports year-over-year
- Keeping written notes of changes

Credit improvement during incarceration is often visible **over time**, not month-to-month.

Documentation matters.

COMMON MISTAKES THAT STALL PROGRESS

Credit maintenance fails most often because of complacency or overreaction. Once a score improves, it is easy to relax discipline. Small details start to feel unimportant. Reports go unchecked. Decisions become less deliberate. Progress slows quietly — not because of a major mistake, but because attention fades.

The opposite problem also occurs. Some people overreact to minor score fluctuations. A small drop — even one caused by normal reporting cycles — triggers impulsive changes. Accounts are closed unnecessarily. New applications are submitted to "fix" the dip. Those reactions often create more instability than the original fluctuation.

Maintenance requires balance. Calm awareness prevents erosion. Measured restraint prevents overcorrection. Stability comes from consistency, not reaction.

Many people unintentionally hurt their credit by:

- Letting others act without oversight
- Ignoring reports because "nothing changed"
- Making emotional decisions after small score drops
- Closing accounts without understanding the impact

Credit discipline is not about reacting. It's about **staying steady**.

THE LONG-GAME MINDSET

Credit is not an event. It's a timeline.

Incarceration, while difficult, provides something many people outside don't have: **time**.

If you avoid damage, allow accounts to age, and stay consistent, time works in your favor.

You are not paused.

You are positioning.

PREPARING FOR WHAT COMES NEXT (WITHOUT JUMPING AHEAD)

Everything you do in this chapter is about setting the **floor**, not the ceiling.

You are:

- Protecting your score
- Preserving options
- Preventing setbacks

Future chapters will address what to do **after release**.

For now, the goal is simple:

Do no harm — and let discipline do the rest.

<u>Why This Matters</u>

Maintenance is where most people fail. Not because they make major mistakes, but because they stop paying attention. Credit damage rarely happens all at once. It happens quietly — through account closures, rising balances, or small lapses in oversight.

For someone incarcerated, neglect is even more dangerous. You do not have daily access to your accounts. You can't fix problems instantly. That means stability must be intentional.

This chapter matters because protecting what you've built is just as important as building it. Time can work in your favor, but only if you avoid unnecessary damage. Maintaining your credit preserves the progress you fought for and ensures that when you step back into society, you ain't starting from behind.

Reflection Questions

1. What does patience mean in credit building?
2. How can slow growth protect me?
3. What temptations could harm my credit?
4. Who can help me responsibly?
5. What does discipline look like now?

Action Steps

- Set realistic credit goals
- Avoid risky authorized user accounts
- Keep balances low
- Monitor consistently

CHAPTER 6 TAKEAWAYS

- Maintenance is active, not passive.
- Inaction can quietly damage credit.
- Account age matters.
- Stability leads to gradual growth.
- Time rewards discipline.

Chapter 7 will focus on **planning for credit success after release**, so the progress you've protected can be used wisely when access returns.

Planning For Credit Success After Release

"The system rewards those who prepare before opportunity shows up."

- Ian Dunlap

WHY PLANNING COMES BEFORE ACTION

Release brings opportunity quickly. Credit offers, financing options, and pressure to "get back on your feet" often arrive before stability does. Without a plan, those opportunities turn into mistakes.

Access creates temptation. The sudden availability of credit can feel like progress, even when it is premature. Planning forces you to separate opportunity from readiness. It ensures that your first financial decisions after release are strategic, not reactive.

This chapter exists to prevent that.

Planning for credit success after release is about **decisions you make before you have access**, not moves you rush into once you do. The goal is to step into freedom with clarity, not confusion.

UNDERSTANDING THE SHIFT THAT HAPPENS AFTER RELEASE

Before release, your focus was:

- Protecting your identity
- Maintaining your score
- Preventing damage

After release, the challenge changes.
You'll face:

- Increased access to credit
- Aggressive marketing and offers
- Emotional pressure to "catch up"
- Advice from people who don't understand credit

Planning allows you to **control the transition** instead of reacting to it.

✓ Previously Learned

Access without discipline creates setbacks, not progress.

DEFINING WHAT "CREDIT SUCCESS" MEANS FOR YOU

Credit success is personal. It should be defined **before** you apply for anything.

Ask yourself:

- What do I need credit *for*, not what do I want it for?
- How will credit support housing, transportation, or employment?
- What outcomes matter in the next 6–12 months?

Your plan should focus on **function**, not status.

SEPARATING NEEDS FROM WANTS

Release brings urgency. After time away, there is a natural desire to rebuild quickly — to replace what was lost, upgrade your environment, and feel normal again. That emotional pressure can blur the line between necessity and impulse.

Credit does not evaluate your intentions. It evaluates your repayment behavior. Using credit for essential stabilization supports your foundation. Using credit to accelerate lifestyle upgrades creates strain before stability is established.

Needs are functional. They support housing, transportation, communication, and employment. Wants are emotional. They often center around comfort, image, or comparison to others. Planning requires honesty about the difference.

The more clearly you define this separation before release, the easier it becomes to resist pressure once access returns.

Needs may include:

- Housing-related expenses
- Reliable transportation
- Utilities or communication

Wants often include:

- Upgrading lifestyle immediately
- Impressing others
- Replacing everything at once

Credit used for wants creates pressure.
Credit used for needs creates stability.

CREATING A CREDIT-FIRST GAME PLAN (ON PAPER)

Before release, your plan should be written, not mental. Planning in your head is not the same as planning on paper. Mental plans are flexible. They shift under pressure. Written plans create accountability. When you define your limits before release, you reduce the likelihood of emotional decisions later.

A credit-first plan means deciding in advance what acceptable terms look like. It means knowing what interest rate you are willing to accept, how many accounts you will open within a set period, and what your priority objectives are. Without defined boundaries, marketing pressure and urgency can influence your choices.

This plan is not about predicting the future perfectly. It is about creating guardrails. Guardrails do not restrict you — they protect you. By committing to structure before access returns, you increase the likelihood that your early decisions after release align with stability instead of impulse.

Your credit plan should include:

- Target credit score ranges
- Types of accounts you intend to pursue (later)
- Maximum acceptable interest rates
- Clear limits on how many accounts you'll open
- A timeline for action, not urgency

Planning on paper reduces emotional decisions.

ANTICIPATING COMMON POST-RELEASE CREDIT TRAPS

Planning means preparing for what will test you. After release, your credit file becomes visible again to lenders, marketers, and financing companies. Many institutions actively target individuals who are rebuilding. The messaging often sounds supportive — "second chance", "easy approval", "no credit needed". But approval does not automatically equal fairness.

Predatory terms are often disguised as opportunity. High interest rates, inflated vehicle pricing, and aggressive payment structures are common in reentry financing environments. The urgency to secure housing or transportation can make these offers feel necessary.

Planning requires awareness of these traps before they appear. When you recognize common patterns — limited-time pressure, guaranteed language, unusually high rates — you are less likely to mistake them for progress. Preparation reduces vulnerability.

Common traps include:

- "Guaranteed approval" offers
- High-interest starter cards
- Buy-here-pay-here auto financing
- Rent-to-own agreements
- Pressure from salespeople to decide immediately

A plan gives you permission to say **no**.

PREPARING YOUR CREDIT PROFILE FOR REVIEW

Before release, assume your credit will be reviewed by:

- Landlords
- Employers (where applicable)
- Utility companies
- Lenders

Planning includes:

- Knowing what your reports currently show
- Understanding weak spots
- Being ready to explain past issues briefly and honestly

Preparation reduces surprises.

ALIGNING CREDIT WITH INCOME REALITY

Credit planning must match income reality, not hope. Why? Because approval does not guarantee affordability. Many lenders evaluate your credit profile more heavily than your actual cash flow. That creates a dangerous gap between what you qualify for and what you can sustainably manage.

After release, income may be unstable at first. Employment transitions, housing adjustments, and reentry expenses create financial fluctuation. Planning for credit without grounding it in realistic income expectations increases the likelihood of strain.

Your credit plan must match your expected cash flow, not your best-case scenario. Conservative estimates protect you. If your income fluctuates, your obligations should remain manageable even during lower-earning months. Stability comes from aligning commitments with predictable resources.

Before release, consider:

- Expected income range
- Employment stability
- Fixed monthly obligations
- Room for credit payments

If credit payments compete with survival expenses, the plan needs adjustment.

✓ Previously Learned

Credit should support your life — not strain it.

ESTABLISHING PERSONAL CREDIT RULES

Discipline is easier when decisions are made in advance. Without personal rules, every offer becomes a new debate. Under pressure, that debate often favors convenience or emotion over long-term stability.

Credit rules function as internal guardrails. They remove negotiation from moments that require clarity. When you define non-negotiables before release, you reduce the risk of impulsive agreements later. Rules do not limit opportunity — they protect it.

Strong credit users ain't disciplined because they have fewer options. They are disciplined because they have standards. Those standards guide behavior when access returns and temptation increases.

Examples:

- "I don't open more than one new account in six months."
- "I don't accept interest rates above ___%."
- "I don't use credit to cover emotional spending."

Rules remove decision-making under pressure.

USING TIME AS AN ADVANTAGE

You don't need to do everything immediately.

Planning recognizes that:

- Credit improves with time.
- Opportunities expand as scores rise.
- Waiting can lead to better terms.

Delayed action is often the smartest action.

TRANSITIONING FROM PLANNING TO EXECUTION (LATER)

This chapter is not about using credit yet.

It's about ensuring that when you do:

- Your moves are intentional.
- Your options are wider.

- Your mistakes are fewer.

Future chapters will address **how to execute the plan responsibly**. For now, planning is the work.

Why This Matters

Reentry is expensive. Housing deposits, transportation, utilities, identification fees, and daily living costs add up quickly. Without financial preparation, even strong motivation can collapse under pressure.

Credit influences how expensive your restart will be. Good credit lowers deposits, reduces interest, and increases approval odds. Poor credit forces you to pay more for everything — sometimes before you even get started.

This chapter matters because preparation reduces panic. When you understand how credit will affect your first 90 days after release, you can plan strategically instead of reacting emotionally. A prepared return home is a controlled return home. Control reduces stress. Reduced stress protects progress.

Reflection Questions

1. What will I need credit for after release?
2. What mistakes do I want to avoid?
3. How will I stick to my plan?
4. What limits should I set?
5. How will I measure success?

Action Steps

- Write your credit plan
- Set rules for applications

- Identify acceptable interest rates
- Create spending boundaries

CHAPTER 7 TAKEAWAYS

- Opportunity comes fast after release.
- Planning protects progress.
- Credit success should be defined in advance.
- Rules prevent emotional decisions.
- Preparation turns access into advantage.

The next chapter will focus on **executing your credit plan responsibly**, so preparation turns into long-term stability — not setbacks.

Executing Your Credit Plan Responsibly After Release

"Execution without discipline is chaos."

- Ian Dunlap

WHEN PLANNING ENDS AND EXECUTION BEGINS

Planning prepares you. Execution tests you.

Execution introduces variables that planning does not fully simulate: emotional pressure, urgency, comparison to others, and the desire to rebuild quickly. Discipline becomes visible at this stage. It is no longer about understanding credit; it is about applying restraint.

After release, credit becomes real very quickly. Applications are approved, offers arrive, and pressure increases. Many people lose control at this stage — not because they lack knowledge, but because they abandon their plan.

This chapter is about **executing your credit plan exactly as designed**, without emotion, urgency, or ego.

THE FIRST RULE OF EXECUTION: FOLLOW THE PLAN

Execution is where most discipline breaks down. Planning feels controlled because there is no immediate pressure. Execution introduces real-world variables — urgency, sales tactics, comparison to others, and the desire to "move fast". That pressure can quietly push you away from the structure you built in Chapter 7.

Your plan exists to protect you from emotional decisions. If you begin negotiating with your own rules the moment you regain access, you undermine the foundation you carefully prepared. Deviating slightly may not feel dangerous at first, but small compromises often lead to larger ones.

Following the plan means honoring the limits you set when you were thinking clearly. It means treating your written boundaries as non-negotiable guardrails, not flexible suggestions.

Execution means:

- Opening only the accounts you planned for
- Ignoring offers you already decided to reject
- Respecting limits you set before release

If a credit opportunity does not fit the plan, it does not deserve your attention.

✓ Previously Learned

Planning removes emotion from decision-making.

MOVING SLOWLY IS A STRATEGY

After release, many people feel pressure to move fast:

- Replace what was lost
- Catch up on time
- Prove progress to others

Credit punishes speed.
Moving too quickly can:

- Lower average account age
- Increase missed payment risk
- Make your profile look unstable

There is no reward for rushing.

USING CREDIT FOR STABILITY, NOT STATUS

After release, identity shifts quickly. There is often an internal pressure to prove progress to yourself and to others. I experienced this personally. Credit can feel like validation. Approvals may feel like momentum. But validation and stability are not the same thing.

Early credit decisions should reinforce your foundation, not your image. When credit is used to secure housing, reliable transportation, or essential utilities, it strengthens independence. When it is used to upgrade lifestyle prematurely, it increases financial strain before income stabilizes.

Status-driven spending often begins subtly: a slightly better car, upgraded electronics, replacing everything at once. These decisions may feel justified, but they create long-term obligations during a period when flexibility is critical. Stability should come first. Comfort and upgrades can follow once consistency is established.

Appropriate early uses may include:

1. Security deposits
2. Transportation-related expenses
3. Utilities or communication needs

Risky uses include:

- Lifestyle upgrades
- Emotional purchases
- Spending to impress others

Credit used for stability creates options.
Credit used for status creates pressure.

RESPONSIBILITY COMES WITH APPROVAL

"Everybody wants the result, but nobody wants the responsibility."

- Nipsey Hussle

Approval is not relief — it is responsibility.

Every balance, payment, and account becomes your obligation, regardless of how easily it was approved.

✓ Previously Learned

Approval does not equal affordability.

MANAGING NEW CREDIT CAREFULLY

The first six to twelve months after opening new accounts are critical. Your behavior during this period establishes the tone of your credit profile moving forward. Lenders and scoring models pay close attention to early patterns. Consistency during this phase builds credibility. Mistakes during this phase create setbacks that take longer to correct.

New credit introduces responsibility immediately. Even small balances require structured tracking. Missing a due date early in your rebuilding phase can undo months of preparation. The goal is not to use credit aggressively — it is to demonstrate control.

Treat every new account as fragile. Until your income stabilizes and your habits are automatic, simplicity is your ally. Fewer accounts, lower balances, and clear tracking systems reduce the risk of error.

If you open new credit accounts:

- Keep balances low

- Pay early, not just on time
- Track due dates manually
- Avoid stacking obligations

Early mistakes are costly and unnecessary.

LEARNING TO SAY NO

Execution is not only about what you agree to — it is about what you decline. After release, you will encounter offers framed as opportunity. Approval may feel like progress. Limits may feel like validation. But every agreement creates obligation.

Saying no is a skill. It protects your plan when pressure rises. Sales language is designed to create urgency and minimize hesitation. Phrases like "limited time", "easy approval", or "you deserve this" are emotional triggers. They are meant to reduce deliberation.

You are not required to accept every opportunity presented to you. Walking away from unfavorable terms strengthens your financial position. Discipline is often invisible in the moment, but it compounds over time.

You may hear:

- "You qualify for more."
- "This offer won't last."
- "You can refinance later."

You do not owe anyone a yes.

Walking away from bad terms is a skill that protects your future.

MONITORING WHILE EXECUTING

Execution does not replace monitoring — it requires it.

Continue to:

- Review statements
- Track balances

- Watch utilization
- Monitor score changes

Problems addressed early stay manageable.

✓ Previously Learned

Small issues ignored become long-term damage.

AVOIDING THE "I'LL FIX IT LATER" TRAP

Many credit problems begin with delay:

- "I'll pay it next month."
- "I'll deal with it once things settle."
- "It's not that serious."

Credit responds poorly to postponement.
Act early.

HABITS DETERMINE OUTCOMES

"The habits you build will either free you or trap you."

- Dr. Claude Anderson

Credit does not track intentions.
It records habits.
Every disciplined action builds momentum.
Every careless action builds resistance.

Why This Matters

Credit is not only about survival; it's about expansion. Once stability is achieved, credit becomes leverage. It can support business formation, investment opportunities, property ownership, and long-term wealth building.

Many people limit their thinking to repair and recovery. They focus only on getting back to neutral. But strong credit allows you to move beyond neutral into growth.

This chapter matters because it reframes credit as a tool for ownership, not just approval. When used responsibly, credit can fund opportunity instead of debt. Understanding this distinction separates survival thinking from strategic thinking. You ain't rebuilding just to exist; you are rebuilding to expand.

Reflection Questions

1. Am I following my plan or reacting emotionally?
2. What pressures could cause mistakes?
3. How do I define responsible execution?
4. What does saying "no" protect?
5. How can I stay disciplined?

Action Steps

- Track new accounts
- Pay early, not late
- Avoid unnecessary credit offers
- Review statements regularly

CHAPTER 8 TAKEAWAYS

- Execution requires discipline.
- Speed increases risk.
- Approval is not obligation.

- Credit should support stability.
- Habits determine long-term outcomes.

The next chapter will focus on **long-term credit management and growth**, so the discipline you apply now continues to compound over time.

Long-Term Credit Management & Growth

"Anybody can get approved. The real skill is keeping your credit strong over time."

- Ian Dunlap

CREDIT SUCCESS IS MEASURED OVER TIME

Reaching a good credit score is not the finish line. Maintaining it — and improving it responsibly — is what determines long-term success.

Many people approach credit improvement as a milestone instead of a long-term system. They celebrate the approval, the score increase, or the new limit — and then gradually relax the habits that made that progress possible. Over time, attention fades. Monitoring becomes less frequent. Balances slowly rise. Discipline weakens.

Strong credit is not built through dramatic moves. It is built through steady, predictable behavior repeated consistently over years. Stability is not maintained by excitement, but by routine.

This chapter focuses on **protecting what you've built and contin-**

uing to grow your credit over time, without undoing years of progress.

SHORT-TERM WINS VS. LONG-TERM STRENGTH

Not all progress carries equal weight. Some improvements feel dramatic but fade quickly. Others build quietly and create durable financial strength over time. Understanding the difference protects you from chasing momentum at the expense of stability.

Short-term wins often feel rewarding because they are visible. An approval notification. A temporary score jump. A new credit line. These moments can create the illusion of rapid advancement. But credit strength is not measured by excitement, it's measured by durability.

Long-term strength is slower and less flashy. It develops through consistent repayment behavior, aging accounts, and restrained expansion. The difference between temporary improvement and lasting strength is patience. When you prioritize durability over excitement, your profile compounds instead of fluctuating.

Short-term credit wins often look like:

- Quick approvals
- Temporary score increases
- Easy access to new accounts

Long-term credit strength is built through:

- Consistent on-time payments
- Low balances maintained over time
- Stable account history
- Controlled growth

Longevity matters more than speed. Why? Because long-term strength is ultimately the long-term win. It just doesn't feel like one in the beginning. Unlike short-term progress, which comes and goes, long-term strength stays with you and continues to work in your favor over time. That's because credit is built on patterns, not moments. Lenders are not impressed by what you did once. They trust what you've proven consistently.

When your profile is built on long-term strength, the benefits become automatic. You're no longer chasing approvals. Approvals start coming to you. You're no longer relying on high-interest options. You qualify for better terms, higher limits, and more flexibility. Opportunities that once felt out of reach become accessible because your profile supports them.

Long-term wins look like stability. They look like a score that holds strong without constant attention. They look like having options: being able to secure funding, housing, or transportation without stress or delay. Most importantly, they look like control and understanding how credit works well enough to maintain and grow it without falling into the same traps that damage it.

This is why long-term strength matters. It doesn't just improve your credit. It changes your position.

✓ Previously Learned

Credit rewards consistency more than intensity.

KEEPING YOUR CREDIT PROFILE STABLE

Stability is one of the most overlooked factors in long-term credit growth.

Strong profiles are built by:

- Keeping older accounts open
- Avoiding unnecessary credit applications
- Allowing accounts to age naturally
- Managing balances conservatively

Frequent changes increase risk. Stability builds trust.

USING CREDIT STRATEGICALLY AS YOU GROW

As your credit improves, your options expand. Growth should be intentional.

Strategic credit growth may include:

- Gradual limit increases without increased spending
- Refinancing high-interest accounts when appropriate
- Upgrading credit products responsibly
- Reducing reliance on debt over time

Growth should simplify your finances, not complicate them.

CREDIT LONGEVITY REQUIRES DAILY DECISIONS

"Good credit isn't built in a moment — it's maintained over a lifetime of decisions."

- Him 500

Credit rarely collapses all at once. It weakens through small, repeated decisions — missed payments, rising balances, or ignored statements.

Long-term success requires attention, even when things seem stable.

MONITORING NEVER STOPS

Long-term credit management depends on consistent monitoring.

Make it a habit to:

- Review your credit reports periodically
- Track balances and utilization
- Watch for unexpected changes
- Address issues immediately

Small problems are easiest to fix when caught early.

✓ Previously Learned

Early detection prevents long-term damage.

AVOIDING LIFESTYLE INFLATION THROUGH CREDIT

As income and stability improve, spending pressure often increases.
Common mistakes include:

- Using credit to maintain appearances
- Letting balances rise alongside income
- Treating available credit as disposable

Strong credit users grow income faster than debt.

THINKING IN YEARS, NOT MONTHS

Long-term credit management means asking:

- Will this decision still make sense next year?
- Does this improve or weaken my options?
- Am I using credit as a tool or a crutch?

Credit decisions should support your future — not borrow from it.

CREDIT AS A LONG-TERM SYSTEM

"Credit is a system. If you don't manage it long-term, it will manage you."

- Dr. Claude Anderson

Credit systems reward structure and discipline. They punish neglect.

Whether credit works quietly for you or loudly against you depends on how consistently you manage it.

Why This Matters

Financial discipline is behavioral, not emotional. Many credit setbacks do not come from lack of knowledge — they come from stress, impulse decisions, or trying to compensate for lost time.

Incarceration can create a "catch-up" mindset after release. That mindset often leads to overspending, unnecessary credit applications, or risky financial moves. Without structure, the desire to move fast becomes self-sabotage.

This chapter matters because emotional control protects financial progress. Credit rewards patience, predictability, and restraint. When you manage your behavior, your score reflects it. Long-term stability requires more than opportunity — it requires discipline.

Reflection Questions

1. What does long-term success mean to me?
2. How can I avoid slipping backward?
3. What habits must stay permanent?
4. How do I handle growth responsibly?
5. What choices affect my future most?

Action Steps

- Keep old accounts open
- Monitor quarterly
- Avoid lifestyle inflation
- Think in years, not months

CHAPTER 9 TAKEAWAYS

- Approval is temporary; management is ongoing.
- Stability supports long-term growth.
- Monitoring must continue.
- Discipline prevents regression.
- Credit longevity creates options.

Chapter 10 will close this book with **encouragement, perspective, and realistic success**, reinforcing why building and protecting credit matters beyond the numbers.

Encouragement, Perspective, and Realistic Success

"You don't have to see the whole staircase, just take the first step."

- Martin Luther King Jr.

FINISHING STRONG MEANS MOVING FORWARD

If you've reached this chapter, you've already done something important: you stayed engaged. You learned how credit works, how to protect it, how to maintain it while incarcerated, and how to plan and execute responsibly after release. You may not be a turd after all.

This chapter is not about tactics. It's about **direction**. Progress does not require perfection. It requires movement… one decision at a time.

PROGRESS IS BUILT IN STEPS, NOT LEAPS

Real change rarely happens all at once. It happens through:

- Small, consistent actions
- Correcting mistakes quickly
- Staying disciplined when it's inconvenient

Credit improvement follows the same pattern. You don't need to do everything immediately. You need to keep moving in the right direction. One of my top sayings is that no action is too small. They all add up over time. That applies here as well. Now, walk that shit down.

✓ Previously Learned

Consistency matters more than intensity.

REDEFINING WHAT SUCCESS LOOKS LIKE

Success is not a single score.

It's not one approval.

It's not a moment.

Success is:

- Stability over time
- Fewer emergencies caused by money
- More options when decisions matter
- Less stress tied to basic needs

Credit is a tool that supports these outcomes, but only when used with intention.

GROWTH IS EXPECTED

"You're supposed to evolve. Don't let anyone convince you otherwise."

- Nipsey Hussle

Your past does not lock you into a future. Growth is not only allowed; it's expected.

As you move forward:

- Your thinking should change.
- Your habits should strengthen.
- Your decisions should become more intentional.

This is not about proving anything to anyone else. It's about building a life that works for you.

Setbacks Do Not Cancel Progress

Mistakes may still happen. A payment may be late. A decision may need correction.

What matters is how you respond.

Progress is protected by:

- Addressing problems early
- Returning to your plan
- Refusing to quit because of one setback

Credit systems forgive correction faster than neglect.

✓ Previously Learned

Small issues handled early prevent long-term damage.

KEEP THE SYSTEM SIMPLE

As life improves, complexity often increases. Resist the urge to over-complicate.

Strong financial systems are built on:

- Clear rules
- Fewer moving parts

- Regular review
- Consistent habits

Simplicity protects momentum.

YOUR RESPONSIBILITY MOVING FORWARD

"Your circumstances may explain your past, but they do not get to decide your future."

- Elijah R. Freeman

This book gave you information, structure, and guidance. What happens next is yours. Responsibility does not mean pressure. It means ownership. Every disciplined choice strengthens your position. Every intentional decision builds confidence. Credit is simply a record of those choices over time. Remember: our future is not dependent upon what we know, but on how well we *apply* what we know.

FINAL TAKEAWAYS

- Progress happens one step at a time.
- Growth is expected, not exceptional.
- Setbacks do not erase effort.
- Discipline protects opportunity.
- Your future is still being written.

You are not behind.
You are not finished.
And you are not defined by where you started.

Success Stories: They Walked So Y'all Could Run

It always seems impossible until it's done...

- Nelson Mandela

Success Story #1

Marcus — "I Refused to Come Home Broke on Paper."

Marcus entered state prison with more fear than anger. Not because of the time (he could handle that), but because of what he didn't know. Bills had been piling up before his arrest. A credit card he barely remembered. A phone bill he never closed. No savings. No plan.

By his second year, Marcus noticed something that bothered him deeply:

Everyone around him was counting down time, but nobody was counting forward. He didn't give a fuck about who went out bad on the yard, who got put on the door, who was blackballed, who was a plate, or if Lil Wayne had more money than Rick Ross. His mind was on freedom, but this was barely talked about.

And when it *was* discussed, it wasn't about apartments, cars, deposits, or how life actually works once the gate opens.

The Turning Point

Marcus overheard a guy on the tier talking about how a former inmate who had been housed in their unit got denied housing after release, strictly because of bad credit. That shook him.

"I realized I could do my time twice — once in prison and once outside — if I didn't fix what was broken on paper."

That night, Marcus made a decision:

If I can't control my body, I'll control my future, he thought.

Step-by-Step: What Marcus Did (From Inside)

1. Ordered His Credit Reports by Mail

He wrote to the credit bureaus using free templates copied by hand. It took weeks. One report arrived. One didn't. He sent it again.

2. Made a List of Every Negative Account

He wrote everything down in a notebook: creditor name, balance, date, status.

3. Disputed Errors First

Some accounts didn't belong to him. Some balances were wrong. He disputed only what he could prove or reasonably question — slow, but clean.

4. Asked for Outside Help (Carefully)

He chose one person he trusted — his sister. No emotion, no pressure. Just facts.

5. Authorized User Strategy

His sister added him to a long-standing, low-balance credit card. He never touched the card. The history did the work.

6. Secured Credit Card Setup

Using saved prison wages and outside help, a secured card was opened in his name. His sister handled payments exactly as Marcus instructed.

7. Stayed Consistent for Over a Year

No missed payments. No new debt. No shortcuts.

Obstacles He Faced

- Mail delays that stretched weeks into months
- Lost dispute letters that had to be resent
- Limited phone time, forcing him to plan conversations ahead
- Trust issues, knowing one mistake by someone else could ruin everything

But Marcus stayed patient. Credit, he learned, rewards discipline, not speed.

The Outcome

While still incarcerated, Marcus reached the low 700s. Not perfect, but good. Solid. Real.

"I'm not going home hoping for a chance. I'm going home with leverage. You don't need freedom to build credit. You need patience, structure, and one reliable outside contact."

Reflective Questions

1. When Marcus realized others were counting down time instead of planning forward, how did that mirror what you see around you right now?
2. What fears do you have about your financial life after release, and which of those fears could be reduced by improving your credit now?
3. Marcus chose one trusted person to help him. Who in your life, if anyone, has proven reliable enough to play that role — and why?
4. If you ordered your credit report today, what do you think you'd find? Errors? Old debt? Nothing at all?
5. Marcus accepted slow progress without quitting. How do you usually respond to delays, lost mail, or setbacks — and how could that response improve?
6. What does "leverage" after release mean to you (housing, transportation, work), and how does credit connect to that vision?
7. What is one small, legal action you could take this month to start building or protecting your credit from where you are?

. . .

Success Story #2

Darnell — "They Tried to Ruin Me While I Was Locked Up."

Darnell's credit wasn't just bad; it was attacked. While he was in federal custody, someone close to him used his information. Bills. Accounts. Missed payments. Collections. By the time he saw his credit report, it felt like someone else had lived his life.

The Turning Point

Darnell didn't explode. He went quiet.

"I realized anger wouldn't fix this. Paper would," he said.

He decided that prison wouldn't be the place where his identity got erased.

Step-by-Step: What Darnell Did:

1. Placed a Fraud Alert and Credit Freeze

Through letters and phone calls, he shut the door on further damage.

2. Documented Everything

Dates. Names. Letters. Copies. He kept a paper trail thicker than the case against him.

3. Disputed Fraudulent Accounts

Slowly. One by one. No rush. No lies.

4. Handled Legit Debts Honestly

Some debts were his. He didn't hide. He arranged payments through a trusted contact.

5. Rebuilt After the Cleanup

Once the bleeding stopped:

- Authorized user on a clean account
- One secured card
- Strict payment rules

Obstacles

- Mail mysteriously "lost"
- Bureau responses delayed
- Phone calls cut short
- Emotional exhaustion from betrayal

But Darnell kept going…

The Outcome

Before release, his score climbed into the high 600s / low 700s.
"They tried to break my name. I rebuilt it."

Takeaway:

Fixing credit from prison starts with stopping the damage then rebuilding with proof.

Reflective Questions

1. Have you experienced financial damage or betrayal while incarcerated? If so, how has that affected your motivation or trust?

2. Darnell shifted from anger to documentation. When you face unfair situations, do you react emotionally or strategically?
3. What steps could you take to protect your identity and credit from further harm while you are still inside?
4. Which debts in your life are truly yours, and which may need to be questioned, verified, or disputed?
5. How comfortable are you asking for help when rebuilding something important, and what fears come up when you think about that?
6. Darnell didn't rebuild until the damage stopped. What "leaks" in your financial life need to be closed first?
7. If someone tried to define you by your worst moment, how would rebuilding your credit help you rewrite that story?

Success Story #3

Trey — "Quiet Preparation Is Power."

Trey didn't talk much. He watched. He saw men come back again and again because nothing changed on the outside. Same debt. Same habits. Same desperation. Same turdful decisions.

<u>The Turning Point</u>

Trey decided his release wouldn't be a question mark. "I wanted my credit working before my feet hit the sidewalk," he said.

<u>Step-by-Step</u>

1. Monthly Credit Review Routine
2. Credit-Builder Loan via Outside Help

3. One Secured Card
4. Zero Missed Payments
5. No Emotional Spending Decisions

<u>Obstacles</u>

- Slow bureaucracy
- Limited communication
- Loneliness
- Doubt

But consistency beat doubt.

<u>The Outcome</u>

Trey came home with good credit, confidence, and options. "Freedom felt different because I planned for it."

Takeaway:

Good credit is built quietly, especially from prison.

<u>Reflective Questions</u>

1. Trey prepared quietly while others focused only on release day. How are you currently using your time, and how could that shift?
2. What does a "stable" life after release look like to you, and how does credit fit into that picture?
3. Trey built routines instead of chasing quick fixes. What routines could you realistically maintain from inside?

4. How do you usually deal with doubt or loneliness, and how might discipline help you push through it?
5. If no one ever praised your efforts until after release, would you still be willing to do the work now? Why or why not?
6. What would it feel like to walk out with credit already working for you instead of against you?
7. What is one habit you can start today that supports long-term financial stability, even if results are not immediate?

The Future Is Built Quietly

The stories of Marcus, Darnell, and Trey are not about luck. They are about decisions made quietly, consistently, and under pressure, just like yours. If you are reading this in a cell, let this be clear: Your future has not stopped just because your movement has. The men in these stories were not special. They were not rich. They were not free. They were patient. They were intentional. And they decided that prison would not be the place where their financial identity died.

Credit is not about money alone. It is about trust, consistency, and proof over time. And here's the truth most people never tell you: The system already expects you to fail after release. It expects your paperwork to be messy. Your credit to be damaged. Your options to be limited. It expects desperation. What it does not expect is preparation.

Every letter you send.

Every account you review.

Every payment made on time through discipline and planning.

Every month you stay consistent, even when nothing seems to change, is a quiet refusal to come home broken.

You may not feel powerful right now. You may feel forgotten. But credit doesn't care about your past; it only records your patterns.

And patterns can be changed…

One day, the door will open. When it does, you will walk out with more than a release date. You will walk out with options. With leverage. With something that speaks for you before you ever open your mouth. That is what this work is really about. Not perfection. Not shortcuts. Not impressing anyone. It's about coming home ready.

So, start where you are. Use what you have. Move slowly but move deliberately. Because freedom feels different when you planned for it.

Reflection Questions

1. How has my thinking changed after reading this book?
2. What belief about myself must change?
3. What fear do I need to release?
4. What does progress look like now?
5. How will I stay committed?

Action Steps

- Write a personal commitment statement
- Review this book regularly
- Share lessons with someone you trust
- Take one step forward each month

** UAD **

Thank you for taking the time to read my guide and I hope that it helps you level up on your credit building journey. Be sure to check out the additional sections, Frequently Asked Questions and the National Reentry Resource Directory, beyond this point to get an even better understanding. Also, if there is a topic that you believe needs to be touched on in my official *How To From Prison* series, reach out to me and let me know. Don't be surprised if you see your suggestions in the back of an *URBAN AINT DEAD* novel under the coming soon section in the future.

Last but not least, if you support us and what we do, request *URBAN AINT DEAD* titles from your people, local bookstores, and prison book distributors. Tell another reader about us and have them do the same. Whether they want urban fiction, urban romance, urban erotica, street lit. or self-help for prisoners, we got them covered. Have your trusted contact get this book so they can read it and use it as a reference. Y'all may not always be able to talk on the phone, but as long as they have this book, you can make sure y'all are on the same page mentally. Thanks in advance and be on the lookout for *How To Build Wealth With Bitcoin From Prison.*

ABOUT THE AUTHOR

Elijah R. Freeman is an author from Riverdale, Georgia and a four-time UBAWA Top 100 Author's award winner. Having penned 14 novels so far, he is quickly becoming known as "The Future of Urban Fiction". He is the C.E.O. of URBAN AINT DEAD and has made some of the biggest moves from behind the wall. His books have appeared in *KITE Magazine*, *States Vs. Us*, *Prison Legal News*, and *Aspiring Authors Magazine*.

25 CREDIT STATISTICS YOU NEVER KNEW

1. Over one in five credit reports contains an error.

Mistakes are common and can lower scores without warning.

2. Payment history makes up about 35% of a credit score.

Missing just one payment can cause major damage.

3. Credit utilization makes up about 30% of a credit score.

High balances hurt more than many people realize.

4. Opening too many accounts in a short time can drop your score.

Lenders see rapid applications as risk.

5. A single late payment can stay on your credit report for up to seven years.
    1. Identity theft is one of the fastest ways credit is destroyed.

Victims often discover damage months or years later.

6. People with higher scores pay thousands less in interest over their lifetime.
    1. Credit scores can affect housing approvals, not just loans.
    2. Some employers check credit reports (where legally allowed).
    3. Medical debt is one of the most common negative items on credit reports.
    4. Closing old accounts can lower your score by reducing credit history length.

7. Car insurance rates can be influenced by credit history in many states.
    1. Most people do not check their credit reports regularly.
    2. Fraud alerts do not stop credit applications — they only warn lenders.
    3. Credit freezes prevent most new accounts from being opened.
    4. Credit reports do not automatically correct themselves.

Errors must be disputed to be removed.

8. High interest rates usually mean low credit scores.
    1. Credit mistakes made early in adulthood often last for years.
    2. Good credit increases financial options, not just borrowing power.
    3. Many identity theft victims are targeted because they can't monitor accounts easily.
    4. Credit scores can change every month based on behavior.
    5. Authorized user accounts can help or hurt depending on how they are managed.

6. Small balances carried over time can cost more than large purchases paid off quickly.
7. Most people underestimate how long it takes to rebuild damaged credit.
8. Strong credit is built through habits, not one-time actions.

Knowledge does not fix credit by itself — but it prevents blind mistakes. Do with this information what you will.

SPECIAL BONUS CHAPTER

THE NEW BBL: BITCOIN BACKED LOANS

A new form of lending has begun to change how people think about credit and borrowing. These are known as Bitcoin Backed Loans (BBLs). Instead of using a credit score as the main qualification, borrowers use their Bitcoin as collateral to receive cash or stable currency without selling their Bitcoin.

This represents a major shift in how lending works. Traditional credit depends on:

- Credit history
- Income verification
- Debt-to-income ratios
- Approval by banks

Bitcoin backed loans depend primarily on:

- How much Bitcoin you own
- The value of that Bitcoin

- Your ability to maintain collateral

This means access to loans can be based on assets instead of credit scores.

What a Bitcoin Backed Loan Is

A Bitcoin backed loan allows a person to:

- Deposit Bitcoin as collateral
- Receive a loan in cash or stablecoin
- Avoid selling their Bitcoin
- Repay the loan over time
- Get their Bitcoin returned after repayment

In simple terms, Bitcoin becomes the new form of security for borrowing.

This is why some people refer to Bitcoin backed loans as the "new BBL" — a new type of borrowing power that does not rely solely on traditional credit systems.

What This Means for the Future of Credit

Bitcoin backed loans introduce a system where:

- Ownership of assets can replace credit history
- Approval is based on value, not background
- Financial access becomes more global
- Banks are no longer the only lenders

This challenges the traditional credit model, which has always required:

- Long histories
- Trust in institutions
- Years of repayment behavior

In the future, credit may become divided into two paths:

- Score-based credit (traditional system)
- Asset-based credit (digital and decentralized systems)

People who hold valuable digital assets may no longer need to rely solely on credit scores to borrow money.

How This Impacts the Credit Game

Bitcoin backed loans change the credit game in several important ways:

- They reduce reliance on credit scores for borrowing.
- They allow people to borrow without creating new debt accounts on credit reports.
- They introduce collateral-based trust instead of reputation-based trust.
- They provide an alternative path to financial access.

However, they also introduce new risks:

- Bitcoin price volatility can cause forced liquidation.
- Borrowers can lose their Bitcoin if values fall.
- These loans are not protected the same way bank loans are.

- Regulation is still developing.

Bitcoin backed loans shift the focus from:
"Can I qualify?"
To
"Can I maintain my collateral?"

Why This Matters to Incarcerated and Reentry Readers

For individuals who have:

- Limited or damaged credit history
- Restricted access to traditional banking
- Difficulty qualifying for loans

Bitcoin backed loans represent a potential future alternative to traditional credit systems.

Instead of rebuilding only through banks and credit cards, some people may eventually:

- Use assets to access capital
- Avoid interest-heavy credit products
- Build financial leverage outside the credit score system

This does not replace credit education, but it adds another layer to the financial landscape readers must understand.

✓ Previously Learned

- Financial systems reward preparation and discipline.

Top Companies Offering Bitcoin Backed Loans

Several companies have developed platforms that allow Bitcoin holders to borrow against their assets. The industry changes frequently, so availability and rules may evolve.

Some of the most well-known providers include:

1. Ledn

Offers Bitcoin backed loans with structured repayment and custody safeguards.

2. Nexo

Provides crypto-collateralized loans with flexible repayment options.

3. Unchained Capital

Focuses on Bitcoin-only lending and long-term custody solutions.

4. Coinbase (Crypto Loans Program – limited availability)

Has offered Bitcoin-collateralized lending through select programs.

5. Abra

Provides asset-backed lending services tied to cryptocurrency holdings.

Note: Availability, regulation, and program details can change. These are examples, not recommendations.

Final Takeaway

- Bitcoin backed loans do not eliminate the need for good credit.

- They expand the definition of borrowing power.
- Traditional credit depends on trust in your history.
- Bitcoin backed loans depend on trust in your assets.
- Buy and hold Bitcoin

In the future, financial success may come from understanding both systems:

- How to protect and grow your credit
- How to protect and manage digital assets

The credit game is changing, and those who understand the shift early will have more options later. More on this in the next installation of this series, *How To Build Wealth With Bitcoin From Prison.*

APPENDICES & TEMPLATES

Appendix A: Credit Report Request Log

Purpose:

To track when and how credit reports are requested while incarcerated.

*Use this log to avoid duplicate requests, missed follow-ups, or confusion over dates.

Bureau	Date Requested	Method (Mail/Helper)	Report Received (Y/N)	Notes
Experian				
Equifax				
TransUnion				

Tip:

Keep this log with copies of all correspondence. Organization protects progress.

Appendix B: Identity Protection Action Checklist

Purpose:

To maintain long-term identity protection while incarcerated.

☐ Credit reports reviewed

☐ Fraud alert placed (if appropriate)

☐ Credit freeze placed (if appropriate)
☐ Outside helpers identified and limited
☐ Documents stored securely
☐ Monitoring schedule established

Note:

Protection is not a one-time action. It is an ongoing system.

Appendix C: Authorized User Safety Checklist

Purpose:

To evaluate whether an authorized user account is helping or hurting your credit.

Before agreeing, confirm:

☐ Primary cardholder has on-time payment history
☐ Balance stays consistently low
☐ You will receive regular updates
☐ You can remove yourself if risk appears

Warning:

Authorized user status helps only when behavior remains disciplined.

Appendix D: Credit Maintenance Habits (Quick Reference)

Purpose:

To reinforce daily and monthly habits that protect credit over time.

Monthly

☐ Review balances
☐ Confirm payments posted
☐ Update tracking logs

Quarterly

☐ Request or review credit report
☐ Check utilization ratios
☐ Confirm account status

Annually

☐ Review overall credit health
☐ Update long-term goals
☐ Adjust strategy if needed

Consistency beats intensity.

Appendix E: Pre-Release Credit Planning Worksheet

Purpose:

To prepare for responsible credit use after release.

Target Credit Goals:

Planned Credit Actions (Future):

Maximum Acceptable Interest Rates:

Personal Credit Rules:

This worksheet should be completed **before** applying for any new credit.

Appendix F: Sample Credit Dispute Letter (General)

(Use only when information is inaccurate or unverifiable)

[Your Name]
[Your Inmate Number]
[Facility Name]
[Facility Address]

Date: __________

To Whom It May Concern,

I am writing to dispute the accuracy of information listed on my credit report.

The following item is inaccurate or can't be verified:

Creditor Name: ____________________

Account Number: ____________________

Reason for Dispute: ________________

Please investigate this matter and provide written confirmation of your findings.

Thank you for your attention to this matter.

Sincerely,
[Your Name]

Important:
Always keep a copy of what you send.

Appendix G: Outside Helper Guidelines

Purpose:
To prevent misunderstandings or misuse of authority.
If someone assists you:

- Provide written instructions
- Limit what they can do
- Require updates
- Never give unrestricted control

Help without structure creates risk.

Appendix H: Recordkeeping & Documentation Checklist

Purpose:
To ensure long-term organization.

☐ Copies of credit reports
☐ Copies of dispute letters
☐ Mailing receipts (if available)
☐ Logs and worksheets
☐ Notes of conversations

Documentation is protection.

Appendix I: Final Reminder to the Reader

Credit improvement is not about perfection.
It is about **attention, discipline, and time**.
Mistakes corrected early stay small.
Habits practiced consistently compound.
Progress maintained patiently becomes opportunity.

USING AN OUTSIDE CONTACT TO LEVERAGE CREDIT KARMA RESPONSIBLY

Here's a clear, responsible framework for how you can use Credit Karma through an outside contact without risking fraud, manipulation, or impulsive decisions.

1. Choose the Right Outside Contact (This Is Critical)

Before you give anyone access to information connected to your name, you need to understand something clearly: this is not about who loves you the most — it's about who is disciplined, stable, and trustworthy under pressure. Credit information is sensitive. It connects to your identity, your future housing, your employment opportunities, and your financial reputation. The wrong person can damage that out of ignorance, emotion, or impulsiveness — even if they mean well. The right person treats this responsibility like handling someone's legal paperwork, not like browsing social media.

To choose correctly, evaluate them using the criteria below:

The outside contact should be someone who is:

- Trustworthy (no history of financial manipulation)
- Stable (not constantly changing phones, emails, or addresses)

- Willing to follow instructions exactly
- Ideally not financially desperate themselves

Best options:

- Parent or grandparent
- Long-term partner or spouse
- Adult child
- Reputable reentry advocate or financial mentor

! Avoid: friends with bad credit habits, anyone who "wants access to the money", or that broke woman you just met that you call your wife because you think if you put a title of assumed prestige on her it'll make her stay down. This is very turdful.

2. Set Up Credit Karma in the Incarcerated Person's Name

This strategy only works if roles are defined from the beginning. The outside contact is not there to "fix" your credit, make executive decisions, or apply for things on your behalf. Their job is limited and specific: observe, report, and communicate. The moment boundaries become unclear, the risk of unauthorized applications, unnecessary inquiries, or even accidental fraud increases. You are building structure, not dependency.

Before any account is created or accessed, agree on the rules below:

- The account must belong to the incarcerated individual, not the outside contact.

Process:
The incarcerated person provides:
Legal name
Date of birth
Social Security number
Current mailing address (can be prison address)
The outside contact:

- Creates the Credit Karma account
- Uses an email created only for this purpose
- Enables two-factor authentication (2FA)

✓ Best Practice

- The incarcerated person keeps a written log of:
- Email address
- Password hint (not full password)
- Security questions

3. Define Clear Boundaries (Put This in Writing).

Setting up Credit Karma (or any monitoring platform) isn't just about entering information and clicking "create account". It requires careful handling because identity theft often begins during setup, especially when personal details are being transmitted between people. Since you're locked up, extra caution must be taken to ensure that login credentials, passwords, and security questions are handled in a way that protects you long term. The goal is transparency without vulnerability.

During the setup process, follow these security principles:

Before anything is checked or applied for, both parties agree that the outside contact MAY:

- Log in and read credit reports
- Take notes or screenshots
- Report changes by mail or phone
- Assist with disputes only with permission

The outside contact MAY NOT:

- Apply for credit
- Accept offers
- Change personal info
- Add themselves as authorized users
- Open bank accounts or cards

✓ Many incarcerated people include this as a written agreement or letter, which builds accountability and trust. Folks can still bullshit you at the end of the day, though. Some people don't give a damn about no piece of paper or their word, especially if they feel like you can't prove it or get entitled. Don't get wiped down.

4. Use Credit Karma for MONITORING — Not SHOPPING

Credit Karma is most powerful when it is used as a window, not a wallet. The platform is designed to show you what lenders are reporting, but it is also designed to tempt users into applying for products. While you're in prison, the objective is not expansion; it is stabilization and protection. Offers, "approval odds", and suggested cards are distractions at this stage. Monitoring means observation, documentation, and restraint.

When reviewing the account, focus only on the following:

Responsible uses:

- Collections
- Charge-offs
- Late payments
- Open accounts
- Incorrect balances

Track:

- Score trends (up/down)
- Report changes

Catch:

- Identity theft
- Old accounts reappearing
- Incorrect personal info

✖ Do not use Credit Karma to apply for cards or loans while incarcerated.

5. Pair Credit Karma With Mail-Based Action

Monitoring without action turns into passive awareness. If your outside contact sees errors, collections, or suspicious changes but nothing is done formally, the problem remains. Because you are incarcerated, official action must flow through documented, mail-based processes that keep authority in your hands. This protects you legally and ensures that nothing is filed or disputed without your approval.

Since prisoners can't click buttons themselves, outside contacts must gather the information and the incarcerated person (you) must take action by mail.

When an issue is identified, take the following steps:

- Dispute letters mailed to bureaus
- Debt validation letters to collectors
- Goodwill letters to original creditors
- Address corrections

✓ This preserves legal control and prevents unauthorized actions.

6. Use Authorized User Strategy (If Appropriate)

The authorized user strategy can either accelerate progress or import someone else's financial mistakes into your profile. From prison, you do not control the primary account holder's behavior — so this move must be calculated, not emotional. It works best when attached to an account that is old, low in balance, and perfectly paid. It fails when attached to someone inconsistent.

If considering this strategy, confirm the following conditions first:

Only if:

- The outside contact has excellent payment history
- Low utilization (<10%)
- No late payments EVER

Rules:

- The incarcerated person is added as authorized user
- No physical card is sent to the prison
- Card is never used by the incarcerated person

- The purpose is reporting benefit only

Credit Karma helps monitor whether the AU account:

- Reports correctly
- Boosts utilization and age
- Appears on all bureaus

7. Monthly Credit Review Routine (Simple & Teachable)

Credit improvement is not a one-time check; it's consistency over time. A structured monthly review creates discipline and prevents small issues from turning into major setbacks. It also trains you in patience and documentation, which are essential skills post-release. The goal is steady monitoring without obsession.

Each month, your review should include:

1. Outside contact logs in
2. Reviews reports
3. Notes:

- Score changes
- New accounts
- Balance changes

4. Sends a written summary by mail

Example summary:

"No new accounts. One collection balance dropped from $1,200 to $900. Score increased 14 points. No disputes needed this month."

✓ This builds financial discipline, patience, and literacy.

8. Teach the Golden Rule

When you rely on someone outside, the temptation is to let them "handle everything". That is how people lose control of their own identity. This system works only if you remain the decision-maker. Information flows to you. Decisions flow from you. That order can't be reversed. Credit Karma is a flashlight, not a steering wheel. It shows what's there — it does not decide what to do next. The Golden Rule of this strategy is reinforced through these principles:

The incarcerated individual:

- Makes the decisions
- Signs the letters
- Chooses the strategy
- Builds patience before release

9. Common Mistakes to Warn Against (Very Important)

Most credit damage in this situation doesn't come from bad intentions — it comes from impatience, excitement, or misplaced trust. Since you can't instantly verify what's happening online, errors can compound before you even know they exist. Prevention is easier than repair.

Avoid these common mistakes:

- Letting someone apply for "easy cards"
- Chasing green approval odds
- Opening accounts too early
- Trusting verbal updates without documentation
- Using Credit Karma scores as "real lender scores"

10. Why This Works (Psychologically & Practically)

This system works because it balances access with discipline. It gives you visibility without giving up control. It builds patience while protecting identity. Most importantly, it creates habits that carry over after release — structured review, cautious decision-making, and delayed gratification.

The long-term benefits include:

- Builds trust with boundaries
- Teaches delayed gratification
- Creates financial agency while incarcerated
- Prevents impulsive credit damage
- Aligns with reentry planning

FREQUENTLY ASKED QUESTIONS (FAQ)

Getting Started

Q: What is credit, and why should I care about it while I'm incarcerated?

A: Credit is your financial reputation; it shows how trustworthy you are as a borrower. Good credit gives you access to better housing, jobs, utilities, and financial products. Taking control of your credit now makes your transition easier when you're released.

Q: What is the difference between a credit report and a credit score?

A: Your credit report lists your financial history — loans, repayments, collections, personal information, and more. Your credit score is a number based on the information in your report that lenders use to judge risk.

Q: Who are the main credit bureaus, and why do they matter to me?

A: The three major bureaus are Experian, Equifax, and TransUnion. They maintain your credit reports and provide them to lenders, landlords, and employers.

Checking Your Credit

Q: How can I get a copy of my credit report from prison?

A: You can request a free copy by mailing a request to AnnualCreditReport.com or directly to the three bureaus. You'll need to include personal information like your full name, date of birth, Social Security number, and your prison mailing address.

Q: What should I look for in my credit report?

A: Verify your personal information, review all listed accounts for accuracy, check for late payments, collections, and unfamiliar accounts that may signal fraud.

Q: How often should I check my credit reports?

A: You are entitled to one free credit report per year from each bureau. Consider requesting one every four months (rotating bureaus) to monitor changes.

Repairing Damaged Credit

Q: How do I fix mistakes I find in my credit report?

A: Mail a written dispute to the bureau that issued the report. List each error, include copies of supporting documents, and send the letter certified mail if possible.

Q: What can I do about debts I can't pay right now?

A: You can try to negotiate with creditors for a payment plan or a "pay for delete" agreement. Some debts may be past the statute of limitations. Focus on debts you can realistically address.

Q: Can I remove negative marks like collections, late payments, or judgments?

A: Negative marks usually stay for seven years, but you can dispute errors or ask creditors for removal (if settled). Bankruptcies remain for up to ten years.

Q: What happens to debts while I'm incarcerated?

A: Debts can still accrue interest and fees. Creditors may send accounts to collections, which may further damage your credit. Consider contacting creditors to explain your situation.

Protecting Your Identity

Q: How can I protect myself from identity theft in prison?

A: Request a fraud alert or credit freeze by mailing the bureaus a written request. Be careful who you share personal information with and store your documents securely.

Q: What if I think someone used my identity while I'm incarcerated?

A: Dispute unauthorized accounts with the bureaus and file a police report if possible. Include documentation proving your incarceration at the time of the fraudulent activity.

Building New Credit

Q: How do I start building credit if I have none or very little?

A: The fastest methods are being added as an authorized user to a family member's existing credit card, opening a secured credit card or a credit builder loan (with help from a friend or family member outside prison), or reporting rent/utility payments if possible.

Q: What is an authorized user, and should I become one?

A: An authorized user is someone added to another person's credit card account. Their positive payment history may be added to your credit report, helping your score, but you're not legally responsible for the debt.

Q: Can I apply for credit, loans, or credit cards from inside prison?

A: Most lenders require proof of income and a physical address, which can limit your options. You may be able to have a trusted outside contact help apply for secured credit products in your name if allowed by the issuer.

Q: What is a secured credit card, and can I get one while incarcerated?

A: A secured credit card requires a cash deposit as collateral. Generally, someone outside prison would need to help with the application and deposit.

Q: Are there credit-building programs inside prison?

A: Some prisons offer financial literacy or credit programs. Check with your counselor or reentry specialist for available resources.

. . .

Maintaining Credit from Prison

Q: How can I keep my credit active and avoid losing it?

A: Keep any existing accounts open and active. If possible, make small payments to show ongoing activity. Ask family or friends to help by paying bills or maintaining accounts.

Q: What happens if accounts go unused while I'm incarcerated?

A: Accounts may be closed due to inactivity, reducing your credit history and opportunity to build a positive record.

Q: Should I close old credit cards I can't use anymore?

A: If there's no fraud risk, it's generally better to keep old accounts open to lengthen your credit history, which helps your score.

Planning for Release

Q: What should I do with my credit upon release?

A: Update your address with the bureaus, request your latest reports to check for changes, start using a secured card or credit builder loan, and pay all bills on time.

Q: What documents will I need to access credit?

A: Secure your Social Security card, birth certificate, state ID, and any correspondence with creditors or bureaus.

Q: How do I establish utilities or rent an apartment with bad or no credit?

A: Be prepared to pay higher deposits or seek co-signers from family or friends. Explain your situation to landlords — some may be willing to work with you.

Special Situations

Q: What is bankruptcy, and should I consider it while in prison?

A: Bankruptcy is a legal process that can erase or reorganize debts. It affects your credit for 7-10 years and may be complicated to file from prison. Seek legal advice before proceeding.

Q: What happens if I co-sign for someone or they co-sign for me?

A: You are both responsible for the debt, and any late payments affect both of your credit reports.

Q: How does incarceration affect my student loans?

A: Federal student loans may be eligible for deferment or rehabilitation. Contact your loan servicer for options.

Q: What should I do about child support or medical debt?

A: These debts can appear on your credit report. Reach out to the relevant agencies to set up payment plans or negotiate reduced payments if eligible.

Legal Rights & Reentry

Q: Do credit bureaus know I'm incarcerated?

A: No, unless you or someone acting on your behalf notifies them. They report only the financial info given to them.

Q: Will my criminal record be included in my credit report?

A: No. Criminal records are not reported on credit files or scores.

Q: What laws protect me from discrimination because of my credit?

A: The Equal Credit Opportunity Act and Fair Credit Reporting Act give you rights for fair lending and access to your credit reports.

Q: What if I need help or legal advice for credit issues?

A: Many organizations offer free credit counseling and legal aid for prisoners and returning citizens. See the resource list in the back of this book.

Miscellaneous

Q: Can I correct errors on my credit report before release?

A: Yes. All dispute and correction processes can be done via mail.

Q: Will building credit help me start a small business?

A: Yes. Many business loans require good personal credit.

Q: Is there a way to build credit without money or help from outside?

A: Progress may be slower, but starting with disputes, protecting your identity, and keeping old accounts open will help until you gain outside support.

. . .

After Release

Q: How quickly can I improve my credit after release?

A: You may begin seeing improvements within months, but large gains usually take 1-2 years of consistent positive behavior.

Q: Should I pay off all my debts right away?

A: Pay what you can, but creating a payment plan and addressing collection accounts systematically can be more sustainable.

Q: How long does it take for credit mistakes to fall off my report?

A: Most negative items fall off after seven years, bankruptcies after up to ten years.

If you have questions not answered here, reach out to the organizations listed in the Resources section or mail the credit bureaus for further guidance. Every effort you make now sets the foundation for a brighter future.

NATIONAL REENTRY RESOURCE DIRECTORY

Why This Directory Matters

Rebuilding your credit begins long before you ever apply for a credit card, loan, or apartment. It begins with stability. Stability means having access to housing, employment, education, and structured support immediately after release. Without these foundational elements, rebuilding credit becomes significantly more difficult.

Many individuals leave prison determined to rebuild their lives but lack access to legitimate opportunities. Without guidance, it is easy to fall into survival mode — working unstable jobs, relying on temporary housing, or operating outside of systems that report positive financial activity. These conditions make it nearly impossible to establish or rebuild credit.

This directory exists to change that.

The organizations listed in this section provide real, structured opportunities designed specifically for returning citizens. These programs help individuals secure housing, obtain employment, learn valuable trades, continue their education, and build financial literacy. Employment and stable housing create the financial activity necessary to establish creditworthiness. Every paycheck earned legitimately and every bill paid on time becomes part of rebuilding your financial identity.

Preparation can and should begin while you are still incarcerated. Many of these programs accept applications from individuals before release. This allows you to transition directly into structured environments that support your growth rather than starting from zero. The more prepared you are before release, the faster you can begin rebuilding your credit and establishing financial independence.

Credit is not just about borrowing money. It is about access. It determines where you can live, what you can finance, what opportunities become available to you, and how much control you have over your future. The faster you establish stability, the faster you can begin rebuilding your credit profile.

This directory serves as a bridge — from incarceration to financial independence.

Use these resources. Apply early. Take advantage of structured programs. Every step forward strengthens your financial future.

Your past does not define your credit. Your actions moving forward do.

State #1: Alabama

Alabama Department of Corrections – Reentry Division

Address: 301 South Ripley Street, Montgomery, AL 36130

Phone: (334) 353-3883

Website: www.doc.alabama.gov

Services Provided: Statewide reentry planning, employment preparation, housing referrals, identification assistance, and transition support

When to Apply: Before release and immediately after release

Eligibility: Individuals releasing from Alabama state prisons

Alabama Career Center System (AlabamaWorks!)

Address: 649 Monroe Street, Montgomery, AL 36131

Phone: (334) 242-8000

Website: www.alabamaworks.alabama.gov

Services Provided: Job placement, resume assistance, workforce training, apprenticeships, and employment referrals

When to Apply: Immediately after release

Eligibility: All Alabama residents, including returning citizens

Aid to Inmate Mothers (AIM)

Address: 1206 4th Avenue North, Birmingham, AL 35203

Phone: (205) 323-4277

Website: www.aidtoinmatemothers.org

Services Provided: Reentry services, employment assistance, housing referrals, mentoring, and family reunification support

When to Apply: Before release and after release

Eligibility: Returning citizens statewide

The Foundry Ministries – Reentry Program

Address: 1800 4th Avenue North, Bessemer, AL 35020

Phone: (205) 424-4673

Website: www.foundryministries.com

Services Provided: Transitional housing, job readiness training, employment placement, financial literacy, and mentoring

When to Apply: Before release and after release

Eligibility: Returning citizens and individuals in recovery

Alabama Department of Labor – Reentry Employment Opportunities

Address: 649 Monroe Street, Montgomery, AL 36131

Phone: (866) 234-5382

Website: www.labor.alabama.gov

Services Provided: Employment placement, job training, career counseling, and workforce development

When to Apply: After release

Eligibility: Returning citizens and Alabama residents

. . .

J.F. Ingram State Technical College (ADOC Technical College)

Address: 5375 Ingram Road, Deatsville, AL 36022

Phone: (334) 290-3200

Website: www.ingramtech.edu

Services Provided: Career technical education, certifications in trades, employment preparation

When to Apply: While incarcerated and after release

Eligibility: Current and formerly incarcerated individuals

Offender Alumni Association (OAA)

Address: 2001 West Street North, Talladega, AL 35160

Phone: (256) 315-4850

Website: www.oaalabama.org

Services Provided: Mentoring, employment assistance, reentry support, community reintegration

When to Apply: Before release and after release

Eligibility: Individuals released from Alabama prisons

Alabama Community College System – Workforce Division

Address: 135 South Union Street, Montgomery, AL 36104

Phone: (334) 293-4500

Website: www.accs.edu

Services Provided: Workforce training, certifications, apprenticeships, and career placement

When to Apply: After release

Eligibility: Alabama residents, including returning citizens

Shelter Care Ministries

Address: 5700 Karl Daly Road, Birmingham, AL 35215

Phone: (205) 836-2557

Website: www.sheltercare.org

Services Provided: Transitional housing, employment assistance, and reentry stabilization

When to Apply: Before release and after release
Eligibility: Returning citizens

Brother Bryan Mission
Address: 1616 2nd Avenue North, Birmingham, AL 35203
Phone: (205) 322-0092
Website: www.brotherbryanmission.com
Services Provided: Emergency housing, job assistance, financial literacy, mentoring
When to Apply: After release
Eligibility: Men returning from incarceration

Firehouse Ministries
Address: 626 2nd Avenue North, Birmingham, AL 35203
Phone: (205) 252-9571
Website: www.firehouseshelter.com
Services Provided: Transitional housing, employment assistance, financial counseling
When to Apply: After release
Eligibility: Returning citizens

Lovelady Center Reentry Program
Address: 7916 2nd Avenue South, Birmingham, AL 35206
Phone: (205) 833-7410
Website: www.loveladycenter.org
Services Provided: Transitional housing, job training, financial literacy, and credit education
When to Apply: Before release and after release
Eligibility: Returning citizens

Alabama Appleseed Center for Law & Justice

Address: 4000 Eagle Point Corporate Drive, Birmingham, AL 35242

Phone: (205) 939-0411

Website: www.alabamaappleseed.org

Services Provided: Legal assistance, expungement guidance, financial reintegration support

When to Apply: After release

Eligibility: Alabama residents with criminal records

Goodwill Industries of Central Alabama – Reentry Services

Address: 2350 Green Springs Highway, Birmingham, AL 35205

Phone: (205) 323-6331

Website: www.goodwillalabama.org

Services Provided: Job training, employment placement, financial literacy programs

When to Apply: After release

Eligibility: Returning citizens

Perry County Reentry Program

Address: 202 Pickens Street, Marion, AL 36756

Phone: (334) 683-6534

Website: Contact local office

Services Provided: Employment assistance, mentoring, housing referrals

When to Apply: After release

Eligibility: Returning citizens

Alabama Department of Human Resources – Family Assistance Division

Address: 50 Ripley Street, Montgomery, AL 36130

Phone: (334) 242-1310

Website: www.dhr.alabama.gov

Services Provided: Financial assistance, housing assistance, food support, stabilization services

When to Apply: After release

Eligibility: Low-income Alabama residents and returning citizens

Catholic Social Services of Montgomery

Address: 4455 Narrow Lane Road, Montgomery, AL 36116

Phone: (334) 288-8890

Website: www.cssalabama.org

Services Provided: Housing assistance, employment assistance, financial counseling

When to Apply: After release

Eligibility: Returning citizens

Salvation Army of Alabama – Reentry Services

Address: 1001 6th Avenue North, Birmingham, AL 35203

Phone: (205) 328-2420

Website: www.salvationarmyalm.org

Services Provided: Transitional housing, employment support, financial counseling

When to Apply: Before release and after release

Eligibility: Returning citizens

United Way of Central Alabama – Reentry Programs

Address: 3600 8th Avenue South, Birmingham, AL 35222

Phone: (205) 458-2200

Website: www.uwca.org

Services Provided: Employment programs, financial literacy, housing referrals

When to Apply: After release

Eligibility: Returning citizens

. . .

Alabama Workforce Innovation and Opportunity Act (WIOA) Program

Address: Multiple statewide locations

Phone: (334) 956-7400

Website: www.alabamaworks.alabama.gov

Services Provided: Job training, employment placement, career counseling

When to Apply: After release

Eligibility: Returning citizens

Volunteers of America Southeast – Reentry Services

Address: 1215 7th Avenue North, Birmingham, AL 35203

Phone: (205) 251-5845

Website: www.voase.org

Services Provided: Housing assistance, employment services, reentry support

When to Apply: Before release and after release

Eligibility: Returning citizens

Alabama Legal Help – Reentry Legal Assistance

Address: Statewide services

Phone: (866) 456-4995

Website: www.alabamalegalhelp.org

Services Provided: Legal assistance, expungement guidance, rights restoration

When to Apply: After release

Eligibility: Alabama residents

West Alabama Works Reentry Program

Address: 1100 21st Street, Tuscaloosa, AL 35401

Phone: (205) 860-1993

Website: www.westalabamaworks.com

Services Provided: Workforce training, employment placement

When to Apply: After release
Eligibility: Returning citizens

Aletheia House Reentry Program
Address: 201 Finley Avenue West, Birmingham, AL 35204
Phone: (205) 324-6502
Website: www.aletheiahouse.com
Services Provided: Transitional housing, employment assistance, financial literacy
When to Apply: Before release and after release
Eligibility: Returning citizens

Community Action Agency of Huntsville/Madison County
Address: 407 Governors Drive SW, Huntsville, AL 35801
Phone: (256) 539-3711
Website: www.hsvca.org
Services Provided: Employment assistance, housing support, financial counseling
When to Apply: After release
Eligibility: Returning citizens

Alabama Power Foundation Workforce Programs
Address: 600 North 18th Street, Birmingham, AL 35203
Phone: (205) 257-1000
Website: www.alabamapowerfoundation.org
Services Provided: Workforce training, employment readiness
When to Apply: After release
Eligibility: Returning citizens

State #2: Alaska

Alaska Department of Corrections – Division of Reentry and Rehabilitation

Address: 550 West 7th Avenue, Suite 1800, Anchorage, AK 99501

Phone: (907) 269-7397

Website: www.doc.alaska.gov

Services Provided: Pre-release planning, employment readiness, housing referrals, identification assistance, and reentry case management

When to Apply: Before release and immediately after release

Eligibility: Individuals releasing from Alaska state correctional facilities

Alaska Department of Labor and Workforce Development – Reentry Employment Services

Address: 3301 Eagle Street, Suite 101, Anchorage, AK 99503

Phone: (907) 269-4800

Website: www.jobs.alaska.gov

Services Provided: Job placement, career counseling, workforce training, resume development, and apprenticeship referrals

When to Apply: After release

Eligibility: Alaska residents, including returning citizens

Alaska Housing Finance Corporation – Reentry Housing Support

Address: 4300 Boniface Parkway, Anchorage, AK 99504

Phone: (907) 338-6100

Website: www.ahfc.us

Services Provided: Housing assistance programs, rental support, and housing referrals

When to Apply: Before release and after release

Eligibility: Low-income Alaska residents, including returning citizens

Volunteers of America Alaska – Reentry Services

Address: 2600 Cordova Street, Suite 100, Anchorage, AK 99503

Phone: (907) 279-9634

Website: www.voaak.org

Services Provided: Transitional housing, employment assistance, case management, and life skills training

When to Apply: Before release and after release

Eligibility: Returning citizens

Anchorage Reentry Coalition

Address: 632 West 6th Avenue, Suite 610, Anchorage, AK 99501

Phone: (907) 786-8900

Website: www.anchoragereentry.org

Services Provided: Reentry planning, employment assistance, mentoring, and housing referrals

When to Apply: Before release and after release

Eligibility: Returning citizens in Anchorage area

Cook Inlet Tribal Council – Reentry and Employment Program

Address: 3600 San Jeronimo Drive, Anchorage, AK 99508

Phone: (907) 793-3600

Website: www.cookinlettribalcouncil.org

Services Provided: Employment placement, vocational training, housing assistance, financial literacy

When to Apply: Before release and after release

Eligibility: Returning citizens and Alaska residents

Alaska Legal Services Corporation – Reentry Legal Assistance

Address: 1016 West 6th Avenue, Suite 200, Anchorage, AK 99501

Phone: (907) 272-9431

Website: www.alsc-law.org

Services Provided: Legal assistance, expungement guidance, housing rights assistance

When to Apply: After release

Eligibility: Low-income Alaska residents and returning citizens

. . .

Nine Star Education and Employment Services

Address: 2533 South Old Knik Road, Wasilla, AK 99654

Phone: (907) 373-7789

Website: www.ninestar.org

Services Provided: Job training, GED preparation, employment placement, workforce readiness

When to Apply: After release

Eligibility: Returning citizens and Alaska residents

Salvation Army Alaska Adult Rehabilitation Program

Address: 3512 Spenard Road, Anchorage, AK 99503

Phone: (907) 276-2898

Website: www.salvationarmyalaska.org

Services Provided: Transitional housing, employment readiness, life skills training

When to Apply: Before release and after release

Eligibility: Returning citizens

Catholic Social Services – Anchorage Reentry Support

Address: 3710 East 20th Avenue, Anchorage, AK 99508

Phone: (907) 222-7300

Website: www.cssalaska.org

Services Provided: Housing assistance, employment support, financial counseling

When to Apply: After release

Eligibility: Returning citizens

Brother Francis Shelter Reentry Support Services

Address: 1021 East 3rd Avenue, Anchorage, AK 99501

Phone: (907) 277-1731

Website: www.cssalaska.org

Services Provided: Emergency housing, employment referrals, reentry stabilization

When to Apply: After release
Eligibility: Returning citizens

Alaska Works Partnership – Apprenticeship and Workforce Training
Address: 161 Klevin Street, Anchorage, AK 99508
Phone: (907) 279-9700
Website: www.alaskaworks.org
Services Provided: Trade training, apprenticeships, employment placement
When to Apply: After release
Eligibility: Alaska residents, including returning citizens

RurAL CAP (Rural Alaska Community Action Program)
Address: 731 East 8th Avenue, Anchorage, AK 99501
Phone: (907) 279-2511
Website: www.ruralcap.org
Services Provided: Housing assistance, employment training, financial literacy programs
When to Apply: After release
Eligibility: Low-income Alaska residents and returning citizens

Alaska Literacy Program – Reentry Education Services
Address: 1840 East Benson Boulevard, Anchorage, AK 99507
Phone: (907) 563-0542
Website: www.alaskaliteracyprogram.org
Services Provided: Education programs, GED preparation, work-force readiness
When to Apply: Before release and after release
Eligibility: Returning citizens

Alaska Native Justice Center – Reentry Support Program

Address: 3201 C Street, Suite 200, Anchorage, AK 99503
Phone: (907) 793-3550
Website: www.anjc.org
Services Provided: Reentry support, employment assistance, housing referrals
When to Apply: Before release and after release
Eligibility: Returning citizens

Alaska Mental Health Trust Authority – Reentry Support Programs

Address: 3745 Community Park Loop, Anchorage, AK 99508
Phone: (907) 269-7960
Website: www.mhtrust.org
Services Provided: Housing assistance, employment support, financial stability programs
When to Apply: After release
Eligibility: Returning citizens

Fairbanks Rescue Mission – Reentry Services

Address: 723 27th Avenue, Fairbanks, AK 99701
Phone: (907) 452-5343
Website: www.fairbanksrescuemission.org
Services Provided: Transitional housing, employment assistance, financial counseling
When to Apply: After release
Eligibility: Returning citizens

Interior Alaska Center for Non-Violent Living – Reentry Support

Address: 726 26th Avenue, Fairbanks, AK 99701
Phone: (907) 452-2293
Website: www.iacnvl.org
Services Provided: Housing assistance, employment support, mentoring

When to Apply: After release
Eligibility: Returning citizens

Alaska Workforce Investment Board
Address: 3301 Eagle Street, Suite 101, Anchorage, AK 99503
Phone: (907) 269-7485
Website: www.awib.alaska.gov
Services Provided: Workforce training, employment assistance, apprenticeships
When to Apply: After release
Eligibility: Alaska residents

Anchorage Gospel Rescue Mission – Reentry Program
Address: 2823 East Tudor Road, Anchorage, AK 99507
Phone: (907) 563-5603
Website: www.anchoragegospelrescuemission.org
Services Provided: Transitional housing, employment readiness, life skills training
When to Apply: After release
Eligibility: Returning citizens

Set Free Alaska – Reentry and Employment Support
Address: 7010 East Bogard Road, Wasilla, AK 99654
Phone: (907) 373-4732
Website: www.setfreealaska.org
Services Provided: Employment training, transitional housing, financial literacy
When to Apply: Before release and after release
Eligibility: Returning citizens

Alaska Community Development Corporation – Workforce Programs

Address: 321 East 5th Avenue, Anchorage, AK 99501

Phone: (907) 258-8722

Website: www.acdcak.org

Services Provided: Job placement, employment readiness, workforce training

When to Apply: After release

Eligibility: Returning citizens

Cook Inlet Housing Authority – Reentry Housing Assistance

Address: 3510 Spenard Road, Anchorage, AK 99503

Phone: (907) 793-3000

Website: www.cookinlethousing.org

Services Provided: Transitional housing, housing assistance programs

When to Apply: After release

Eligibility: Returning citizens

Alaska Reentry Partnership Anchorage

Address: 632 West 6th Avenue, Anchorage, AK 99501

Phone: (907) 786-8900

Website: Contact local office

Services Provided: Reentry planning, employment referrals, housing assistance

When to Apply: Before release and after release

Eligibility: Returning citizens

State #3: Arizona

Arizona Department of Corrections, Rehabilitation & Reentry (ADCRR) – Community Reentry Division

Address: 1601 West Jefferson Street, Phoenix, AZ 85007

Phone: (602) 542-5497

Website: www.azcorrections.gov

Services Provided: Pre-release planning, employment readiness, identification assistance, community supervision support

When to Apply: Before release and immediately after release

Eligibility: Individuals releasing from Arizona state prisons

Arizona Department of Economic Security (DES) – Employment Services

Address: 1789 West Jefferson Street, Phoenix, AZ 85007

Phone: (602) 542-4248

Website: www.azdes.gov

Services Provided: Job placement, workforce training, resume assistance, WIOA programs

When to Apply: After release

Eligibility: Arizona residents, including returning citizens

Arizona@Work (Statewide Workforce Network)

Address: Multiple statewide locations

Phone: (602) 771-2222

Website: www.arizonaatwork.com

Services Provided: Employment placement, career counseling, apprenticeships, workforce development

When to Apply: Immediately after release

Eligibility: Returning citizens and Arizona residents

A New Leaf – Reentry Services

Address: 868 East University Drive, Mesa, AZ 85203

Phone: (480) 969-4024

Website: www.turnanewleaf.org

Services Provided: Transitional housing, employment services, financial literacy, case management

When to Apply: Before release and after release

Eligibility: Returning citizens

. . .

Chicanos Por La Causa (CPLC) – Reentry Employment Program

Address: 1112 East Buckeye Road, Phoenix, AZ 85034

Phone: (602) 257-0700

Website: www.cplc.org

Services Provided: Job placement, vocational training, housing referrals, financial coaching

When to Apply: Before release and after release

Eligibility: Returning citizens statewide

Catholic Charities Community Services – Reentry Support

Address: 4747 North 7th Avenue, Phoenix, AZ 85013

Phone: (602) 285-1999

Website: www.catholiccharitiesaz.org

Services Provided: Housing assistance, employment support, financial counseling

When to Apply: After release

Eligibility: Returning citizens

St. Joseph the Worker – Employment Assistance Program

Address: 2826 South 16th Street, Phoenix, AZ 85034

Phone: (602) 275-6242

Website: www.sjwjobs.org

Services Provided: Job placement, resume support, interview preparation, workforce training

When to Apply: After release

Eligibility: Returning citizens and low-income residents

Arizona Center for Empowerment (ACE)

Address: 2305 North 16th Street, Phoenix, AZ 85006

Phone: (602) 414-0909

Website: www.azcend.org

Services Provided: Workforce training, housing assistance, financial education

When to Apply: After release
Eligibility: Returning citizens

Goodwill of Central & Northern Arizona – Reentry Workforce Program

Address: 515 North 51st Avenue, Phoenix, AZ 85043
Phone: (602) 535-4444
Website: www.goodwillaz.org
Services Provided: Job training, employment placement, financial literacy programs
When to Apply: After release
Eligibility: Returning citizens

Fresh Start Women's Foundation – Reentry Financial Services

Address: 1130 East McDowell Road, Phoenix, AZ 85006
Phone: (602) 252-8494
Website: www.freshstartwomen.org
Services Provided: Financial literacy education, employment training, credit counseling
When to Apply: After release
Eligibility: Returning citizens (women only)

Salvation Army Southwest Division – Reentry Housing Support

Address: 2707 East Van Buren Street, Phoenix, AZ 85008
Phone: (602) 267-4100
Website: www.salvationarmyphoenix.org
Services Provided: Transitional housing, employment assistance, financial counseling
When to Apply: Before release and after release
Eligibility: Returning citizens

Community Bridges, Inc. – Reentry Stabilization Services

Address: 1855 East Southern Avenue, Mesa, AZ 85204
Phone: (877) 931-9142
Website: www.communitybridgesaz.org
Services Provided: Housing referrals, employment support, reentry case management
When to Apply: Before release and after release
Eligibility: Returning citizens

Arizona Justice Project – Legal Reentry Assistance
Address: 1401 East Jefferson Street, Phoenix, AZ 85034
Phone: (602) 496-0286
Website: www.azjusticeproject.org
Services Provided: Legal assistance, post-conviction support, rights restoration guidance
When to Apply: After release
Eligibility: Arizona residents with criminal records

Friendly House – Workforce and Financial Empowerment Program
Address: 113 West Sherman Street, Phoenix, AZ 85003
Phone: (602) 257-1870
Website: www.friendlyhouse.org
Services Provided: Employment training, financial literacy education, housing referrals
When to Apply: After release
Eligibility: Returning citizens

UMOM New Day Centers – Reentry Housing Support
Address: 3333 East Van Buren Street, Phoenix, AZ 85008
Phone: (602) 275-7852
Website: www.umom.org
Services Provided: Transitional housing, employment readiness, financial stability programs

When to Apply: After release
Eligibility: Returning citizens

Phoenix Rescue Mission – Changing Lives Center
Address: 338 North 15th Avenue, Phoenix, AZ 85007
Phone: (602) 233-3000
Website: www.phoenixrescuemission.org
Services Provided: Transitional housing, job training, financial literacy programs
When to Apply: After release
Eligibility: Returning citizens

Arizona Community Action Association – Financial Empowerment Services
Address: 340 East Palm Lane, Suite 315, Phoenix, AZ 85004
Phone: (602) 604-0640
Website: www.azcaa.org
Services Provided: Financial literacy, budgeting education, housing stabilization
When to Apply: After release
Eligibility: Low-income residents and returning citizens

Arizona Builders Alliance – Apprenticeship & Workforce Training
Address: 1700 East Thomas Road, Suite 200, Phoenix, AZ 85016
Phone: (602) 274-8222
Website: www.azbuilders.org
Services Provided: Construction apprenticeships, trade certifications, job placement
When to Apply: After release
Eligibility: Arizona residents, including returning citizens

Arizona Self-Help – Financial Coaching Program

Address: 3454 North 51st Avenue, Phoenix, AZ 85031

Phone: (602) 841-1160

Website: www.azselfhelp.org

Services Provided: Financial coaching, budgeting education, credit-building assistance

When to Apply: After release

Eligibility: Returning citizens

Catholic Community Services of Southern Arizona – Reentry Support

Address: 140 West Speedway Boulevard, Tucson, AZ 85705

Phone: (520) 623-0344

Website: www.ccs-soaz.org

Services Provided: Housing assistance, employment support, financial counseling

When to Apply: After release

Eligibility: Returning citizens

Pima County One-Stop Career Center – Reentry Employment Services

Address: 2797 East Ajo Way, Tucson, AZ 85713

Phone: (520) 724-2646

Website: www.pima.gov

Services Provided: Job placement, workforce training, resume development

When to Apply: After release

Eligibility: Returning citizens

Maricopa County Human Services Department – Reentry Programs

Address: 234 North Central Avenue, Phoenix, AZ 85004

Phone: (602) 506-5911

Website: www.maricopa.gov

Services Provided: Housing support, employment referrals, financial assistance programs

When to Apply: After release

Eligibility: Returning citizens

Arizona Women's Education & Employment (AWEE)

Address: 640 North 1st Avenue, Phoenix, AZ 85003

Phone: (602) 223-4333

Website: www.awee.org

Services Provided: Job training, financial literacy education, credit coaching

When to Apply: After release

Eligibility: Returning citizens

Tucson Urban League – Workforce Development Program

Address: 2305 South Park Avenue, Tucson, AZ 85713

Phone: (520) 791-9522

Website: www.tucsonurbanleague.org

Services Provided: Employment placement, financial literacy, housing referrals

When to Apply: After release

Eligibility: Returning citizens

Arizona Department of Housing – Housing Stability Programs

Address: 1110 West Washington Street, Suite 280, Phoenix, AZ 85007

Phone: (602) 771-1000

Website: www.housing.az.gov

Services Provided: Housing assistance programs, rental stabilization, housing referrals

When to Apply: After release

Eligibility: Low-income Arizona residents and returning citizens

. . .

State #4: Arkansas

Arkansas Department of Corrections – Reentry Services Division

Address: 6814 Princeton Pike, Pine Bluff, AR 71602

Phone: (870) 267-6999

Website: www.doc.arkansas.gov

Services Provided: Pre-release planning, housing referrals, employment preparation, identification assistance

When to Apply: Before release and immediately after release

Eligibility: Individuals releasing from Arkansas state correctional facilities

Arkansas Division of Community Correction – Reentry Program

Address: 105 West Capitol Avenue, Little Rock, AR 72201

Phone: (501) 682-9510

Website: www.doc.arkansas.gov/community-correction

Services Provided: Transitional housing referrals, supervision support, employment readiness

When to Apply: Before release and after release

Eligibility: Returning citizens under supervision or release

Arkansas Division of Workforce Services

Address: 2 Capitol Mall, Little Rock, AR 72201

Phone: (501) 682-2121

Website: www.dws.arkansas.gov

Services Provided: Job placement, workforce training, resume assistance, career development

When to Apply: Immediately after release

Eligibility: Arkansas residents, including returning citizens

Our House Transitional Housing Program

Address: 302 East Roosevelt Road, Little Rock, AR 72206

Phone: (501) 374-7383

Website: www.ourhouseshelter.org

Services Provided: Transitional housing, employment services, financial literacy, job readiness training

When to Apply: Before release and after release

Eligibility: Returning citizens and individuals facing housing instability

Goodwill Industries of Arkansas – Reentry Employment Program

Address: 1110 West 7th Street, Little Rock, AR 72201

Phone: (501) 372-5100

Website: www.goodwillar.org

Services Provided: Job training, employment placement, career readiness programs

When to Apply: After release

Eligibility: Returning citizens and individuals with criminal records

Central Arkansas Reentry Coalition (CARE Coalition)

Address: 3805 West 12th Street, Little Rock, AR 72204

Phone: (501) 444-2273

Website: www.arkansasreentry.com

Services Provided: Mentorship, housing referrals, employment assistance, community reintegration

When to Apply: Before release and after release

Eligibility: Returning citizens in Central Arkansas

Restore Hope Arkansas – Reentry and Workforce Initiative

Address: 610 East Emma Avenue, Springdale, AR 72764

Phone: (479) 443-7714

Website: www.restorehopear.org

Services Provided: Workforce development, reentry planning, housing referrals, employment coordination

When to Apply: Before release and after release

Eligibility: Returning citizens statewide

. . .

Arkansas Department of Human Services – Transitional Support Services

Address: 700 Main Street, Little Rock, AR 72201

Phone: (501) 682-1001

Website: www.humanservices.arkansas.gov

Services Provided: Financial assistance, housing support, employment referrals

When to Apply: After release

Eligibility: Returning citizens and low-income residents

Quality Living Center Reentry Program

Address: 3925 Asher Avenue, Little Rock, AR 72204

Phone: (501) 663-3490

Website: www.qualitylivingcenter.net

Services Provided: Transitional housing, employment support, reentry case management

When to Apply: Before release and after release

Eligibility: Returning citizens

Pathway to Freedom (GYST House)

Address: 8101 Frenchman Lane, Little Rock, AR 72209

Phone: (501) 568-1682

Website: www.gysthouseinc.com

Services Provided: Reentry housing, employment readiness, mentoring

When to Apply: Before release and after release

Eligibility: Returning citizens

Lighthouse Mission Ministries – Nehemiah Program

Address: 2400 Confederate Boulevard, Little Rock, AR 72206

Phone: (501) 374-5399

Website: www.lhmm.org

Services Provided: Housing support, employment readiness, life skills training

When to Apply: After release

Eligibility: Returning citizens

Arkansas Adult Learning Resource Center

Address: 124 West Capitol Avenue, Suite 1000, Little Rock, AR 72201

Phone: (501) 907-2490

Website: www.aalrc.org

Services Provided: GED preparation, adult education, workforce readiness

When to Apply: Before release and after release

Eligibility: Returning citizens

Arkansas Career Education Division

Address: 1 Commerce Way, Little Rock, AR 72202

Phone: (501) 682-1970

Website: www.arcareereducation.org

Services Provided: Trade certifications, workforce training, employment preparation

When to Apply: Before release and after release

Eligibility: Returning citizens

Arkansas Community Action Agencies (Statewide Network)

Address: Multiple locations statewide

Phone: (501) 372-0807

Website: www.arkansascommunityaction.org

Services Provided: Employment assistance, housing support, financial literacy education

When to Apply: After release

Eligibility: Returning citizens and low-income residents

. . .

Better Community Development, Inc. – Empowerment Center

Address: 2905 King Street, Little Rock, AR 72206

Phone: (501) 663-4774

Website: www.bcdinc.org

Services Provided: Employment assistance, job training, financial counseling

When to Apply: After release

Eligibility: Returning citizens

University of Arkansas at Little Rock – Community-Based Reentry Initiative

Address: 2801 South University Avenue, Little Rock, AR 72204

Phone: (501) 569-8000

Website: www.ualr.edu

Services Provided: Mentoring, workforce readiness, reentry education programs

When to Apply: Before release and after release

Eligibility: Returning citizens

Arkansas Workforce Centers (Statewide Locations)

Address: Multiple locations statewide

Phone: (855) 225-4440

Website: www.arjoblink.arkansas.gov

Services Provided: Job placement, career training, resume support

When to Apply: After release

Eligibility: Returning citizens

Arkansas 211 Reentry Support Line

Address: Statewide resource

Phone: 211

Website: www.arkansas211.org

Services Provided: Referrals for housing, employment, financial assistance

When to Apply: Before release and after release

Eligibility: Returning citizens

Prison Fellowship – Arkansas Reentry Program

Address: 4411 North Shore Drive, North Little Rock, AR 72118

Phone: (501) 945-4516

Website: www.prisonfellowship.org

Services Provided: Mentorship, housing support, employment readiness

When to Apply: Before release and after release

Eligibility: Returning citizens

Second Chance Arkansas – Reentry Assistance Network

Address: Statewide services

Phone: Contact via website

Website: www.secondchanceguide.com

Services Provided: Housing referrals, employment assistance, financial reintegration programs

When to Apply: Before release and after release

Eligibility: Returning citizens

Arkansas Department of Commerce – Workforce Development Programs

Address: 1 Commerce Way, Little Rock, AR 72202

Phone: (501) 682-1121

Website: www.arkansascommerce.com

Services Provided: Workforce training, employment assistance, apprenticeship programs

When to Apply: After release

Eligibility: Returning citizens

. . .

City of Little Rock Reentry Program

Address: 500 West Markham Street, Little Rock, AR 72201

Phone: (501) 371-4510

Website: www.littlerock.gov

Services Provided: Employment support, housing referrals, reentry coordination

When to Apply: After release

Eligibility: Returning citizens

InnerChange Freedom Initiative Arkansas

Address: Tucker Unit, 2400 State Farm Road, Tucker, AR 72168

Phone: (501) 842-0375

Website: www.prisonfellowship.org

Services Provided: Employment readiness, mentoring, reentry preparation

When to Apply: Before release and after release

Eligibility: Returning citizens

Arkansas Legal Aid – Reentry Legal Support

Address: 714 South Main Street, Jonesboro, AR 72401

Phone: (800) 952-9243

Website: www.arlegalaid.org

Services Provided: Legal aid, record sealing assistance, employment barrier removal

When to Apply: After release

Eligibility: Returning citizens

State #5: California

California Department of Corrections and Rehabilitation – Division of Rehabilitative Programs

Address: 1515 S Street, Sacramento, CA 95811

Phone: (916) 324-7308

Website: www.cdcr.ca.gov

Services Provided: Pre-release planning, employment readiness, housing referrals, identification assistance

When to Apply: Before release and immediately after release

Eligibility: Individuals releasing from California state prisons

California Prison Industry Authority (CALPIA)

Address: 560 East Natoma Street, Folsom, CA 95630

Phone: (916) 358-1767

Website: www.calpia.ca.gov

Services Provided: Vocational training, trade certifications, employment preparation

When to Apply: Before release and after release

Eligibility: Incarcerated and formerly incarcerated individuals

California Workforce Development Board

Address: 800 Capitol Mall, Suite 1022, Sacramento, CA 95814

Phone: (916) 657-1440

Website: www.cwdb.ca.gov

Services Provided: Job placement, apprenticeships, WIOA-funded training

When to Apply: After release

Eligibility: California residents, including returning citizens

America's Job Center of California (AJCC)

Address: Multiple statewide locations

Phone: (916) 654-7799

Website: www.edd.ca.gov

Services Provided: Employment placement, resume development, career counseling

When to Apply: Immediately after release

Eligibility: Returning citizens

. . .

Center for Employment Opportunities (CEO)

Address: 1125 Benton Street, Santa Clara, CA 95050

Phone: (408) 508-6441

Website: www.ceoworks.org

Services Provided: Immediate transitional employment, job coaching, financial stability planning

When to Apply: Immediately after release

Eligibility: Individuals recently released from incarceration

Homeboy Industries

Address: 130 West Bruno Street, Los Angeles, CA 90012

Phone: (323) 526-1254

Website: www.homeboyindustries.org

Services Provided: Job training, employment placement, financial literacy, case management

When to Apply: After release

Eligibility: Returning citizens

Anti-Recidivism Coalition

Address: 1320 East 7th Street, Suite 260, Los Angeles, CA 90021

Phone: (213) 955-5885

Website: www.antirecidivism.org

Services Provided: Employment support, mentorship, housing referrals

When to Apply: Before release and after release

Eligibility: Returning citizens statewide

The Fortune Society West

Address: Los Angeles, CA (Regional Services)

Phone: (213) 943-3450

Website: www.fortunesociety.org

Services Provided: Housing referrals, employment support, reentry planning

When to Apply: Before release and after release
Eligibility: Returning citizens

Volunteers of America Los Angeles
Address: 3600 Wilshire Boulevard, Suite 1500, Los Angeles, CA 90010
Phone: (213) 389-1500
Website: www.voala.org
Services Provided: Transitional housing, employment services, financial literacy
When to Apply: Before release and after release
Eligibility: Returning citizens

Goodwill Southern California
Address: 342 North San Fernando Road, Los Angeles, CA 90031
Phone: (323) 539-2000
Website: www.goodwillsocal.org
Services Provided: Job training, employment placement, financial education
When to Apply: After release
Eligibility: Returning citizens

Catholic Charities of California
Address: 1100 K Street, Sacramento, CA 95814
Phone: (916) 492-9417
Website: www.cacatholic.org
Services Provided: Housing assistance, financial counseling, employment support
When to Apply: After release
Eligibility: Returning citizens

Legal Services for Prisoners with Children

Address: 1540 Market Street, Suite 490, San Francisco, CA 94102
Phone: (415) 255-7036
Website: www.prisonerswithchildren.org
Services Provided: Legal support, record expungement guidance, employment barrier removal
When to Apply: After release
Eligibility: Returning citizens (with children)

Rubicon Programs
Address: 2500 Bissell Avenue, Richmond, CA 94804
Phone: (510) 412-8200
Website: www.rubiconprograms.org
Services Provided: Employment placement, financial coaching, housing stabilization
When to Apply: After release
Eligibility: Returning citizens

California Department of Housing and Community Development
Address: 2020 West El Camino Avenue, Sacramento, CA 95833
Phone: (916) 263-2911
Website: www.hcd.ca.gov
Services Provided: Housing assistance programs, rental support, housing referrals
When to Apply: After release
Eligibility: Low-income residents and returning citizens

Second Chance Program
Address: 6144 University Avenue, Suite 210, San Diego, CA 92115
Phone: (619) 234-8888
Website: www.secondchanceprogram.org
Services Provided: Employment readiness, housing support, financial literacy

When to Apply: After release
Eligibility: Returning citizens

California Reentry Program
Address: Multiple statewide locations
Phone: (800) 410-0599
Website: www.calreentry.com
Services Provided: Transitional housing, employment assistance
When to Apply: Before release and after release
Eligibility: Returning citizens

Five Keys Schools and Programs
Address: 70 Oak Grove Street, San Francisco, CA 94107
Phone: (415) 734-3310
Website: www.fivekeys.org
Services Provided: GED, vocational education, workforce readiness
When to Apply: Before release and after release
Eligibility: Returning citizens

Center for Restorative Justice Works
Address: Oakland, CA
Phone: (510) 394-5632
Website: www.crjw.org
Services Provided: Reentry coordination, mentoring, employment support
When to Apply: Before release and after release
Eligibility: Returning citizens

San Francisco Adult Probation Department Reentry Division
Address: 945 Bryant Street, San Francisco, CA 94103
Phone: (415) 553-1706

Website: www.sfgov.org/adultprobation

Services Provided: Housing referrals, employment support, supervision services

When to Apply: Upon release

Eligibility: Individuals under supervision

Los Angeles Regional Reentry Partnership

Address: 211 West Temple Street, Los Angeles, CA 90012

Phone: (213) 974-7600

Website: www.lacounty.gov

Services Provided: Reentry coordination, housing referrals, employment assistance

When to Apply: Before release and after release

Eligibility: Returning citizens

California Community Colleges Chancellor's Office

Address: 1102 Q Street, Sacramento, CA 95811

Phone: (916) 445-8752

Website: www.cccco.edu

Services Provided: Trade certifications, associate degrees, workforce training

When to Apply: After release

Eligibility: Returning citizens

Root & Rebound

Address: 1730 Franklin Street, Suite 300, Oakland, CA 94612

Phone: (510) 279-4662

Website: www.rootandrebound.org

Services Provided: Legal education, employment rights guidance, housing rights support

When to Apply: Before release and after release

Eligibility: Returning citizens

. . .

Urban League of Greater Los Angeles

Address: 3450 Mount Vernon Drive, Los Angeles, CA 90008

Phone: (323) 299-3181

Website: www.urbanleaguela.org

Services Provided: Employment placement, financial literacy, workforce development

When to Apply: After release

Eligibility: Returning citizens

Bay Area Community Resources

Address: 171 Carlos Drive, San Rafael, CA 94903

Phone: (415) 755-2328

Website: www.bacr.org

Services Provided: Employment assistance, mentoring, financial education

When to Apply: After release

Eligibility: Returning citizens

State #7: Connecticut

Connecticut Department of Correction – Reentry and Transitional Services Unit

Address: 24 Wolcott Hill Road, Wethersfield, CT 06109

Phone: (860) 692-7780

Website: www.portal.ct.gov/DOC

Services Provided: Pre-release planning, employment readiness, housing referrals, identification assistance

When to Apply: Before release and immediately after release

Eligibility: Individuals releasing from Connecticut state correctional facilities

Connecticut Department of Labor

Address: 200 Folly Brook Boulevard, Wethersfield, CT 06109

Phone: (860) 263-6000

Website: www.ctdol.state.ct.us

Services Provided: Employment placement, workforce training, apprenticeships, resume assistance

When to Apply: After release

Eligibility: Connecticut residents, including returning citizens

American Job Centers Connecticut

Address: Multiple statewide locations

Phone: (860) 263-6000

Website: www.ctdol.state.ct.us/ajc

Services Provided: Job placement, career counseling, employment readiness training

When to Apply: Immediately after release

Eligibility: Returning citizens

Connecticut Reentry Collaborative

Address: Statewide services

Phone: (860) 263-6000

Website: www.ctreentry.org

Services Provided: Reentry coordination, employment support, housing referrals

When to Apply: Before release and after release

Eligibility: Returning citizens

The WorkPlace

Address: 350 Fairfield Avenue, Bridgeport, CT 06604

Phone: (203) 610-8500

Website: www.workplace.org

Services Provided: Job training, employment placement, workforce readiness

When to Apply: After release

Eligibility: Returning citizens

. . .

Career Resources, Inc.

Address: 350 Fairfield Avenue, Bridgeport, CT 06604

Phone: (203) 576-7001

Website: www.careerresources.org

Services Provided: Employment assistance, career training, job placement

When to Apply: After release

Eligibility: Returning citizens

Community Partners in Action

Address: 110 Bartholomew Avenue, Hartford, CT 06106

Phone: (860) 566-2030

Website: www.cpa-ct.org

Services Provided: Reentry support, employment readiness, housing assistance

When to Apply: Before release and after release

Eligibility: Returning citizens

The Connection, Inc.

Address: 100 Roscommon Drive, Suite 203, Middletown, CT 06457

Phone: (860) 343-5500

Website: www.theconnectioninc.org

Services Provided: Transitional housing, employment assistance, reentry case management

When to Apply: Before release and after release

Eligibility: Returning citizens

Goodwill of Western and Northern Connecticut

Address: 165 Ocean Terrace, Bridgeport, CT 06605

Phone: (203) 368-6511

Website: www.gwct.org

Services Provided: Job training, employment placement, financial literacy education

When to Apply: After release

Eligibility: Returning citizens

Catholic Charities Archdiocese of Hartford

Address: 331 Main Street, Norwich, CT 06360

Phone: (860) 889-8346

Website: www.ccarchdiocese.org

Services Provided: Housing assistance, employment support, financial counseling

When to Apply: After release

Eligibility: Returning citizens

Chrysalis Center

Address: 255 Homestead Avenue, Hartford, CT 06112

Phone: (860) 263-4400

Website: www.chrysaliscenterct.org

Services Provided: Transitional housing, employment assistance, financial literacy

When to Apply: Before release and after release

Eligibility: Returning citizens

New Haven Reentry Initiative

Address: 232 Farnam Street, New Haven, CT 06510

Phone: (203) 946-6935

Website: www.newhavenct.gov

Services Provided: Employment support, housing referrals, mentoring

When to Apply: Before release and after release

Eligibility: Returning citizens

. . .

Urban League of Southern Connecticut

Address: 745 Main Street, Bridgeport, CT 06604

Phone: (203) 366-0141

Website: www.ulsc.org

Services Provided: Employment placement, financial literacy education, housing referrals

When to Apply: After release

Eligibility: Returning citizens

Connecticut Legal Services

Address: 62 Washington Street, Middletown, CT 06457

Phone: (860) 344-0380

Website: www.ctlegal.org

Services Provided: Legal assistance, record expungement guidance, employment barrier removal

When to Apply: After release

Eligibility: Returning citizens

Workforce Alliance

Address: 560 Ella T. Grasso Boulevard, New Haven, CT 06519

Phone: (203) 867-4030

Website: www.workforcealliance.biz

Services Provided: Job training, employment placement, workforce readiness

When to Apply: After release

Eligibility: Returning citizens

Columbus House

Address: 586 Ella T. Grasso Boulevard, New Haven, CT 06519

Phone: (203) 401-4400

Website: www.columbushouse.org

Services Provided: Transitional housing, employment support, financial stability programs

When to Apply: After release
Eligibility: Returning citizens

Connecticut Fair Housing Center
Address: 60 Popieluszko Court, Hartford, CT 06106
Phone: (860) 247-4400
Website: www.ctfairhousing.org
Services Provided: Housing assistance, housing rights education
When to Apply: After release
Eligibility: Returning citizens

United Way of Connecticut
Address: 30 Laurel Street, Hartford, CT 06106
Phone: (860) 571-7500
Website: www.unitedwayinc.org
Services Provided: Housing referrals, employment assistance, financial literacy programs
When to Apply: After release
Eligibility: Returning citizens

Operation Fresh Start Connecticut
Address: Hartford, CT
Phone: (860) 522-7400
Website: Contact via local offices
Services Provided: Employment readiness, mentoring, financial literacy education
When to Apply: After release
Eligibility: Returning citizens

Connecticut Community Colleges
Address: 61 Woodland Street, Hartford, CT 06105
Phone: (860) 493-0000

Website: www.ct.edu

Services Provided: Trade certifications, degree programs, workforce training

When to Apply: After release

Eligibility: Returning citizens

Open Hearth Association

Address: 437 Sheldon Street, Hartford, CT 06106

Phone: (860) 525-3447

Website: www.theopenhearth.org

Services Provided: Transitional housing, employment assistance, financial education

When to Apply: After release

Eligibility: Returning citizens

211 Connecticut Reentry Support Line

Address: Statewide service

Phone: 211

Website: www.211ct.org

Services Provided: Referrals for housing, employment, financial assistance

When to Apply: Before release and after release

Eligibility: Returning citizens

State #8: Delaware

Delaware Department of Correction – Bureau of Reentry Services

Address: 245 McKee Road, Dover, DE 19904

Phone: (302) 739-5601

Website: www.doc.delaware.gov

Services Provided: Pre-release planning, employment readiness, housing referrals, identification assistance

When to Apply: Before release and immediately after release

Eligibility: Individuals releasing from Delaware state correctional facilities

Delaware Department of Labor

Address: 4425 North Market Street, Wilmington, DE 19802

Phone: (302) 761-8000

Website: www.labor.delaware.gov

Services Provided: Job placement, workforce training, apprenticeships, career counseling

When to Apply: Immediately after release

Eligibility: Delaware residents, including returning citizens

Delaware JobLink Career Centers

Address: Multiple statewide locations

Phone: (302) 761-8085

Website: www.joblink.delaware.gov

Services Provided: Employment placement, resume assistance, job training

When to Apply: After release

Eligibility: Returning citizens

Delaware Center for Justice

Address: 100 West 10th Street, Suite 1002, Wilmington, DE 19801

Phone: (302) 658-7174

Website: www.dcjustice.org

Services Provided: Reentry support, employment assistance, mentoring, financial literacy

When to Apply: Before release and after release

Eligibility: Returning citizens

Connections Community Support Programs

Address: 500 West 10th Street, Wilmington, DE 19801

Phone: (302) 984-1400
Website: www.connectionscsp.org
Services Provided: Transitional housing, employment support, case management
When to Apply: Before release and after release
Eligibility: Returning citizens

Goodwill of Delaware and Delaware County
Address: 300 East Lea Boulevard, Wilmington, DE 19802
Phone: (302) 761-4640
Website: www.goodwillde.org
Services Provided: Job training, employment placement, financial literacy programs
When to Apply: After release
Eligibility: Returning citizens

West End Neighborhood House
Address: 710 North Lincoln Street, Wilmington, DE 19805
Phone: (302) 658-4171
Website: www.wenh.org
Services Provided: Employment assistance, housing support, financial literacy education
When to Apply: After release
Eligibility: Returning citizens

Delaware Housing Authority
Address: 18 The Green, Dover, DE 19901
Phone: (302) 739-4263
Website: www.destatehousing.com
Services Provided: Housing assistance, rental support, housing referrals
When to Apply: After release
Eligibility: Low-income residents and returning citizens

. . .

Catholic Charities of the Diocese of Wilmington

Address: 2601 West 4th Street, Wilmington, DE 19805

Phone: (302) 655-9624

Website: www.cdow.org

Services Provided: Housing assistance, employment support, financial counseling

When to Apply: After release

Eligibility: Returning citizens

Salvation Army Delaware

Address: 400 North Orange Street, Wilmington, DE 19801

Phone: (302) 652-1601

Website: www.salvationarmyde.org

Services Provided: Transitional housing, employment readiness, financial literacy

When to Apply: After release

Eligibility: Returning citizens

First State Community Action Agency

Address: 308 North Railroad Avenue, Georgetown, DE 19947

Phone: (302) 856-7761

Website: www.firststatecaa.org

Services Provided: Employment training, housing support, financial literacy

When to Apply: After release

Eligibility: Returning citizens

Delaware Opportunities Industrialization Center

Address: 625 North Orange Street, Wilmington, DE 19801

Phone: (302) 762-3777

Website: www.doic.org

Services Provided: Job training, employment placement, career development

When to Apply: After release

Eligibility: Returning citizens

Urban League of Metropolitan Wilmington

Address: 1007 North Orange Street, Wilmington, DE 19801

Phone: (302) 658-5624

Website: www.urbanleagueofwilmington.org

Services Provided: Employment placement, financial literacy, housing referrals

When to Apply: After release

Eligibility: Returning citizens

Delaware Community Legal Aid Society

Address: 100 West 10th Street, Suite 801, Wilmington, DE 19801

Phone: (302) 575-0660

Website: www.declasi.org

Services Provided: Legal assistance, record expungement guidance, housing rights support

When to Apply: After release

Eligibility: Returning citizens

Tri-State Community Action Agency

Address: 201 Booth Street, Elkton, MD 21921 (serves Delaware residents)

Phone: (410) 398-4063

Website: www.tri-statecaa.org

Services Provided: Housing assistance, employment training, financial education

When to Apply: After release

Eligibility: Returning citizens

. . .

Kingswood Community Center

Address: 2300 Bowers Street, Wilmington, DE 19802

Phone: (302) 764-9022

Website: www.kingswoodcommunitycenter.org

Services Provided: Employment assistance, financial literacy, mentoring

When to Apply: After release

Eligibility: Returning citizens

Delaware Technical Community College

Address: 400 Stanton Christiana Road, Newark, DE 19713

Phone: (302) 454-3900

Website: www.dtcc.edu

Services Provided: Trade certifications, workforce training, degree programs

When to Apply: After release

Eligibility: Returning citizens

YWCA Delaware

Address: 100 West 10th Street, Suite 705, Wilmington, DE 19801

Phone: (302) 655-0039

Website: www.ywcade.org

Services Provided: Housing support, employment readiness, financial literacy

When to Apply: After release

Eligibility: Returning citizens

Ministry of Caring

Address: 115 East 14th Street, Wilmington, DE 19801

Phone: (302) 652-5523

Website: www.ministryofcaring.org

Services Provided: Transitional housing, employment support, financial education

When to Apply: After release
Eligibility: Returning citizens

211 Delaware Reentry Support Line
Address: Statewide service
Phone: 211
Website: www.delaware211.org
Services Provided: Referrals for housing, employment, financial assistance
When to Apply: Before release and after release
Eligibility: Returning citizens

State #9: Florida

Florida Department of Corrections – Reentry Services Division
Address: 501 South Calhoun Street, Tallahassee, FL 32399
Phone: (850) 488-7052
Website: www.dc.state.fl.us
Services Provided: Pre-release planning, employment readiness, housing referrals, identification assistance
When to Apply: Before release and immediately after release
Eligibility: Individuals releasing from Florida state prisons

Florida Department of Economic Opportunity
Address: 107 East Madison Street, Tallahassee, FL 32399
Phone: (850) 245-7105
Website: www.floridajobs.org
Services Provided: Job placement, workforce training, apprenticeships, employment counseling
When to Apply: Immediately after release
Eligibility: Florida residents, including returning citizens

CareerSource Florida

Address: Multiple statewide locations
Phone: (850) 921-1119
Website: www.careersourceflorida.com
Services Provided: Job placement, resume development, workforce training
When to Apply: After release
Eligibility: Returning citizens

Operation New Hope
Address: 1830 North Main Street, Jacksonville, FL 32206
Phone: (904) 354-4673
Website: www.operationnewhope.org
Services Provided: Employment placement, job training, transitional housing assistance
When to Apply: Before release and after release
Eligibility: Returning citizens

The Fortune Society Florida
Address: Orlando, FL
Phone: (407) 245-0012
Website: www.fortunesociety.org
Services Provided: Employment assistance, housing referrals, financial literacy
When to Apply: Before release and after release
Eligibility: Returning citizens

Goodwill Industries of Florida
Address: Multiple statewide locations
Phone: (407) 235-1541
Website: www.goodwillfl.org
Services Provided: Job training, employment placement, financial literacy programs
When to Apply: After release

Eligibility: Returning citizens

Florida Rights Restoration Coalition

Address: 2930 West Colonial Drive, Orlando, FL 32808

Phone: (407) 801-4350

Website: www.floridarrc.com

Services Provided: Employment support, mentoring, financial literacy education

When to Apply: After release

Eligibility: Returning citizens

Salvation Army Florida

Address: Multiple statewide locations

Phone: (800) 725-2769

Website: www.salvationarmyflorida.org

Services Provided: Transitional housing, employment readiness, financial counseling

When to Apply: Before release and after release

Eligibility: Returning citizens

Catholic Charities Florida

Address: Multiple statewide locations

Phone: (850) 222-2180

Website: www.catholiccharitiesusa.org

Services Provided: Housing assistance, employment support, financial literacy

When to Apply: After release

Eligibility: Returning citizens

CareerSource Central Florida

Address: 4360 West Colonial Drive, Orlando, FL 32808

Phone: (407) 531-1227

Website: www.careersourcecentralflorida.com

Services Provided: Job placement, workforce training, career counseling

When to Apply: After release

Eligibility: Returning citizens

Miami-Dade Corrections and Rehabilitation Reentry Services

Address: 2525 Northwest 62nd Street, Miami, FL 33147

Phone: (786) 263-7000

Website: www.miamidade.gov

Services Provided: Employment support, housing referrals, reentry planning

When to Apply: Before release and after release

Eligibility: Returning citizens

Broward Sheriff's Office Reentry Program

Address: 2601 West Broward Boulevard, Fort Lauderdale, FL 33312

Phone: (954) 831-5900

Website: www.sheriff.org

Services Provided: Employment readiness, mentoring, housing referrals

When to Apply: Before release and after release

Eligibility: Returning citizens

Palm Beach County Reentry Program

Address: 205 North Dixie Highway, West Palm Beach, FL 33401

Phone: (561) 355-2381

Website: www.pbcgov.org

Services Provided: Employment assistance, housing referrals, mentoring

When to Apply: After release

Eligibility: Returning citizens

. . .

Florida Housing Finance Corporation

Address: 227 North Bronough Street, Tallahassee, FL 32301

Phone: (850) 488-4197

Website: www.floridahousing.org

Services Provided: Housing assistance programs, rental support

When to Apply: After release

Eligibility: Returning citizens

Urban League of Broward County

Address: 560 Northwest 27th Avenue, Fort Lauderdale, FL 33311

Phone: (954) 584-0777

Website: www.ulbroward.org

Services Provided: Employment placement, financial literacy, workforce training

When to Apply: After release

Eligibility: Returning citizens

Jacksonville Reentry Center

Address: 1024 Superior Street, Jacksonville, FL 32254

Phone: (904) 630-2365

Website: www.jacksonville.gov

Services Provided: Housing referrals, employment support, reentry planning

When to Apply: After release

Eligibility: Returning citizens

Transition, Inc.

Address: 1735 Dr. Martin Luther King Jr Street North, St. Petersburg, FL 33704

Phone: (727) 895-3309

Website: www.transitioninc.org

Services Provided: Employment readiness, financial literacy, housing referrals

When to Apply: After release

Eligibility: Returning citizens

Florida Legal Services

Address: 2425 Torreya Drive, Tallahassee, FL 32303

Phone: (850) 385-7900

Website: www.floridalegal.org

Services Provided: Legal assistance, expungement guidance, employment barrier removal

When to Apply: After release

Eligibility: Returning citizens

211 Florida Reentry Support Line

Address: Statewide service

Phone: 211

Website: www.211.org

Services Provided: Referrals for housing, employment, financial assistance

When to Apply: Before release and after release

Eligibility: Returning citizens

Second Chance Center Florida

Address: Orlando, FL

Phone: (407) 245-0012

Website: Contact via local offices

Services Provided: Employment readiness, mentoring, housing referrals

When to Apply: After release

Eligibility: Returning citizens

. . .

Florida Community College System

Address: Multiple statewide locations

Phone: (850) 245-0407

Website: www.fldoe.org

Services Provided: Trade certifications, workforce training, degree programs

When to Apply: After release

Eligibility: Returning citizens

Tampa Bay Reentry Coalition

Address: Tampa, FL

Phone: (813) 221-2315

Website: Contact local office

Services Provided: Employment support, housing referrals, mentoring

When to Apply: After release

Eligibility: Returning citizens

State #11: Hawaii

Hawaii Department of Corrections and Rehabilitation – Reentry Services Branch

Address: 1177 Alakea Street, Honolulu, HI 96813

Phone: (808) 587-1288

Website: www.dcr.hawaii.gov

Services Provided: Pre-release planning, employment readiness, housing referrals, identification assistance

When to Apply: Before release and immediately after release

Eligibility: Individuals releasing from Hawaii state correctional facilities

Hawaii Department of Labor and Industrial Relations

Address: 830 Punchbowl Street, Honolulu, HI 96813

Phone: (808) 586-8844

Website: www.labor.hawaii.gov

Services Provided: Job placement, workforce training, apprenticeships, employment counseling

When to Apply: Immediately after release

Eligibility: Hawaii residents, including returning citizens

American Job Center Hawaii

Address: Multiple statewide locations

Phone: (808) 586-8877

Website: www.hirenethawaii.com

Services Provided: Job placement, resume development, workforce training

When to Apply: After release

Eligibility: Returning citizens

Hawaii Workforce Development Council

Address: 830 Punchbowl Street, Room 417, Honolulu, HI 96813

Phone: (808) 586-8630

Website: www.labor.hawaii.gov/wdc

Services Provided: Workforce training, apprenticeships, career counseling

When to Apply: After release

Eligibility: Returning citizens

Goodwill Hawaii

Address: 2610 Kilihau Street, Honolulu, HI 96819

Phone: (808) 836-0313

Website: www.goodwillhawaii.org

Services Provided: Job training, employment placement, financial literacy education

When to Apply: After release

Eligibility: Returning citizens

. . .

Catholic Charities Hawaii

Address: 1822 Keeaumoku Street, Honolulu, HI 96822

Phone: (808) 527-4777

Website: www.catholiccharitieshawaii.org

Services Provided: Housing assistance, employment support, financial counseling

When to Apply: Before release and after release

Eligibility: Returning citizens

The Institute for Human Services

Address: 546 Kaaahi Street, Honolulu, HI 96817

Phone: (808) 447-2800

Website: www.ihshawaii.org

Services Provided: Transitional housing, employment assistance, financial stability programs

When to Apply: After release

Eligibility: Returning citizens

Helping Hands Hawaii

Address: 2100 North Nimitz Highway, Honolulu, HI 96819

Phone: (808) 536-7234

Website: www.helpinghandshawaii.org

Services Provided: Employment assistance, housing referrals, financial literacy education

When to Apply: After release

Eligibility: Returning citizens

Hawaii Housing Finance and Development Corporation

Address: 677 Queen Street, Suite 300, Honolulu, HI 96813

Phone: (808) 587-0620

Website: www.hhfdc.hawaii.gov

Services Provided: Housing assistance programs, rental support

When to Apply: After release

Eligibility: Returning citizens

Hawaii Legal Aid Society

Address: 924 Bethel Street, Honolulu, HI 96813

Phone: (808) 536-4302

Website: www.legalaidhawaii.org

Services Provided: Legal assistance, expungement guidance, employment barrier removal

When to Apply: After release

Eligibility: Returning citizens

University of Hawaii Community Colleges

Address: 2444 Dole Street, Honolulu, HI 96822

Phone: (808) 956-8111

Website: www.hawaii.edu

Services Provided: Trade certifications, workforce training, degree programs

When to Apply: After release

Eligibility: Returning citizens

Pu'a Foundation

Address: Honolulu, HI

Phone: (808) 521-1787

Website: www.puafoundation.org

Services Provided: Reentry support, employment readiness, mentoring

When to Apply: Before release and after release

Eligibility: Returning citizens

TJ Mahoney & Associates Reentry Services

Address: Honolulu, HI

Phone: (808) 561-5414

Website: Contact local office

Services Provided: Employment assistance, mentoring, financial literacy education

When to Apply: After release

Eligibility: Returning citizens

Hawaii Community Action Program

Address: 1132 Bishop Street, Suite 100, Honolulu, HI 96813

Phone: (808) 521-4531

Website: www.hcapweb.org

Services Provided: Housing assistance, employment support, financial education

When to Apply: After release

Eligibility: Returning citizens

Salvation Army Hawaii

Address: 2950 Manoa Road, Honolulu, HI 96822

Phone: (808) 988-2136

Website: www.salvationarmyhawaii.org

Services Provided: Transitional housing, employment readiness, financial counseling

When to Apply: Before release and after release

Eligibility: Returning citizens

Hawaii Literacy

Address: 1130 North Nimitz Highway, Suite A-217, Honolulu, HI 96817

Phone: (808) 537-6706

Website: www.hawaiiliteracy.org

Services Provided: Education programs, workforce readiness, employment training

When to Apply: After release

Eligibility: Returning citizens

. . .

Alu Like, Inc.

Address: 458 Keawe Street, Honolulu, HI 96813

Phone: (808) 535-6700

Website: www.alulike.org

Services Provided: Job training, employment placement, workforce readiness

When to Apply: After release

Eligibility: Returning citizens

211 Hawaii Reentry Support Line

Address: Statewide service

Phone: 211

Website: www.auw211.org

Services Provided: Referrals for housing, employment, financial assistance

When to Apply: Before release and after release

Eligibility: Returning citizens

Hawaii Urban League

Address: Honolulu, HI

Phone: (808) 524-4309

Website: Contact local office

Services Provided: Employment assistance, financial literacy education, mentoring

When to Apply: After release

Eligibility: Returning citizens

Department of Human Services Hawaii

Address: 1390 Miller Street, Honolulu, HI 96813

Phone: (808) 586-4993

Website: www.humanservices.hawaii.gov

Services Provided: Financial assistance, housing support, employment referrals

When to Apply: After release

Eligibility: Returning citizens

State #12: Idaho

Idaho Department of Correction – Reentry and Community Services Division

Address: 1299 North Orchard Street, Suite 110, Boise, ID 83706

Phone: (208) 658-2000

Website: www.idoc.idaho.gov

Services Provided: Pre-release planning, employment readiness, housing referrals, identification assistance

When to Apply: Before release and immediately after release

Eligibility: Individuals releasing from Idaho state correctional facilities

Idaho Department of Labor

Address: 317 West Main Street, Boise, ID 83735

Phone: (208) 332-3570

Website: www.labor.idaho.gov

Services Provided: Job placement, workforce training, apprenticeships, career counseling

When to Apply: Immediately after release

Eligibility: Idaho residents, including returning citizens

Idaho American Job Centers

Address: Multiple statewide locations

Phone: (208) 332-3570

Website: www.labor.idaho.gov/job-seekers

Services Provided: Employment placement, resume development, career readiness training

When to Apply: After release

Eligibility: Returning citizens

Idaho Reentry Services Program

Address: Boise, ID

Phone: (208) 658-2000

Website: www.idoc.idaho.gov

Services Provided: Reentry planning, employment referrals, housing assistance

When to Apply: Before release and after release

Eligibility: Returning citizens

Goodwill Industries of Idaho

Address: 1463 South Federal Way, Boise, ID 83705

Phone: (208) 375-4687

Website: www.goodwillidaho.org

Services Provided: Job training, employment placement, financial literacy education

When to Apply: After release

Eligibility: Returning citizens

Idaho Housing and Finance Association

Address: 565 West Myrtle Street, Boise, ID 83702

Phone: (208) 331-4700

Website: www.idahohousing.com

Services Provided: Housing assistance programs, rental support, housing referrals

When to Apply: After release

Eligibility: Returning citizens

Salvation Army Idaho

Address: 9492 West Emerald Street, Boise, ID 83704

Phone: (208) 343-5429

Website: www.salvationarmyboise.org

Services Provided: Transitional housing, employment readiness, financial counseling

When to Apply: Before release and after release

Eligibility: Returning citizens

Catholic Charities of Idaho

Address: 725 South 9th Street, Boise, ID 83702

Phone: (208) 345-6031

Website: www.ccidaho.org

Services Provided: Housing assistance, employment support, financial literacy

When to Apply: After release

Eligibility: Returning citizens

Idaho Legal Aid Services

Address: 1447 South Tyrell Lane, Boise, ID 83706

Phone: (208) 746-7541

Website: www.idaholegalaid.org

Services Provided: Legal assistance, record expungement guidance, employment barrier removal

When to Apply: After release

Eligibility: Returning citizens

Boise Rescue Mission Ministries

Address: 308 South 24th Street, Boise, ID 83702

Phone: (208) 343-2389

Website: www.boiserm.org

Services Provided: Transitional housing, employment readiness, financial literacy programs

When to Apply: After release

Eligibility: Returning citizens

. . .

Idaho Community Action Network

Address: 3450 Hill Road, Boise, ID 83702

Phone: (208) 331-9089

Website: www.idahocan.org

Services Provided: Housing assistance, employment support, financial education

When to Apply: After release

Eligibility: Returning citizens

College of Western Idaho Workforce Development

Address: 1760 West University Drive, Boise, ID 83725

Phone: (208) 562-3000

Website: www.cwi.edu

Services Provided: Workforce training, trade certifications, employment readiness

When to Apply: After release

Eligibility: Returning citizens

Idaho Workforce Development Council

Address: 317 West Main Street, Boise, ID 83735

Phone: (208) 332-3570

Website: www.wdc.idaho.gov

Services Provided: Apprenticeships, employment training, workforce readiness

When to Apply: After release

Eligibility: Returning citizens

Jesse Tree Housing Assistance

Address: 1121 West Miller Street, Boise, ID 83702

Phone: (208) 383-9486

Website: www.jessetreeidaho.org

Services Provided: Housing assistance, eviction prevention, financial education

When to Apply: After release
Eligibility: Returning citizens

Idaho Youth Ranch Workforce Development
Address: 5465 West Irving Street, Boise, ID 83706
Phone: (208) 378-2610
Website: www.youthranch.org
Services Provided: Job training, employment placement, workforce readiness
When to Apply: After release
Eligibility: Returning citizens

United Way of Treasure Valley
Address: 720 West Washington Street, Boise, ID 83702
Phone: (208) 336-1070
Website: www.unitedwaytv.org
Services Provided: Housing referrals, employment assistance, financial literacy programs
When to Apply: After release
Eligibility: Returning citizens

Idaho Department of Health and Welfare
Address: 450 West State Street, Boise, ID 83702
Phone: (208) 334-5500
Website: www.healthandwelfare.idaho.gov
Services Provided: Financial assistance, housing support, employment referrals
When to Apply: After release
Eligibility: Returning citizens

St. Vincent de Paul Idaho
Address: 6464 West State Street, Boise, ID 83714

Phone: (208) 331-2208
Website: www.svdpid.org
Services Provided: Transitional housing, employment assistance, financial counseling
When to Apply: After release
Eligibility: Returning citizens

Idaho Community Colleges System
Address: Multiple statewide locations
Phone: (208) 332-6800
Website: www.boardofed.idaho.gov
Services Provided: Trade certifications, degree programs, work-force training
When to Apply: After release
Eligibility: Returning citizens

211 Idaho Reentry Support Line
Address: Statewide service
Phone: 211
Website: www.211.idaho.gov
Services Provided: Referrals for housing, employment, financial assistance
When to Apply: Before release and after release
Eligibility: Returning citizens

State #13: Illinois

Illinois Department of Corrections – Reentry Services Division
Address: 1301 Concordia Court, Springfield, IL 62794
Phone: (217) 558-2200
Website: www.idoc.illinois.gov
Services Provided: Pre-release planning, employment readiness, housing referrals, identification assistance
When to Apply: Before release and immediately after release

Eligibility: Individuals releasing from Illinois state correctional facilities

Illinois Department of Employment Security

Address: 33 South State Street, Chicago, IL 60603

Phone: (800) 244-5631

Website: www.ides.illinois.gov

Services Provided: Job placement, workforce training, career counseling

When to Apply: Immediately after release

Eligibility: Illinois residents, including returning citizens

American Job Centers Illinois

Address: Multiple statewide locations

Phone: (877) 342-7533

Website: www.illinoisjoblink.com

Services Provided: Employment placement, resume development, workforce training

When to Apply: After release

Eligibility: Returning citizens

Safer Foundation

Address: 571 West Jackson Boulevard, Chicago, IL 60661

Phone: (312) 922-2200

Website: www.saferfoundation.org

Services Provided: Employment placement, job training, financial literacy education

When to Apply: Before release and after release

Eligibility: Returning citizens

Illinois Department of Human Services

Address: 100 South Grand Avenue East, Springfield, IL 62762

Phone: (800) 843-6154

Website: www.dhs.state.il.us

Services Provided: Financial assistance, housing support, employment referrals

When to Apply: After release

Eligibility: Returning citizens

St. Leonard's Ministries

Address: 2100 West Warren Boulevard, Chicago, IL 60612

Phone: (312) 738-1414

Website: www.slministries.org

Services Provided: Transitional housing, employment readiness, financial literacy

When to Apply: Before release and after release

Eligibility: Returning citizens

Howard Area Community Center

Address: 7648 North Paulina Street, Chicago, IL 60626

Phone: (773) 262-6622

Website: www.howardarea.org

Services Provided: Employment assistance, housing referrals, financial education

When to Apply: After release

Eligibility: Returning citizens

Heartland Alliance

Address: 208 South LaSalle Street, Suite 1300, Chicago, IL 60604

Phone: (312) 660-1300

Website: www.heartlandalliance.org

Services Provided: Housing assistance, employment support, financial literacy

When to Apply: After release

Eligibility: Returning citizens

. . .

Goodwill Industries of Metropolitan Chicago

Address: 6054 South Western Avenue, Chicago, IL 60636

Phone: (773) 627-5400

Website: www.goodwillmetrochicago.org

Services Provided: Job training, employment placement, workforce readiness

When to Apply: After release

Eligibility: Returning citizens

Chicago Cook Workforce Partnership

Address: 69 West Washington Street, Chicago, IL 60602

Phone: (312) 603-0200

Website: www.chicookworks.org

Services Provided: Job placement, career counseling, workforce training

When to Apply: After release

Eligibility: Returning citizens

Illinois Housing Development Authority

Address: 111 East Wacker Drive, Chicago, IL 60601

Phone: (312) 836-5200

Website: www.ihda.org

Services Provided: Housing assistance programs, rental support

When to Apply: After release

Eligibility: Returning citizens

Catholic Charities of the Archdiocese of Chicago

Address: 721 North LaSalle Street, Chicago, IL 60654

Phone: (312) 655-7700

Website: www.catholiccharities.net

Services Provided: Housing assistance, employment support, financial counseling

When to Apply: After release

Eligibility: Returning citizens

The Fortune Society Illinois

Address: Chicago, IL

Phone: (312) 555-1212

Website: www.fortunesociety.org

Services Provided: Employment readiness, mentoring, housing referrals

When to Apply: After release

Eligibility: Returning citizens

Illinois Legal Aid Online

Address: 161 North Clark Street, Chicago, IL 60601

Phone: (312) 347-5700

Website: www.illinoislegalaid.org

Services Provided: Legal assistance, expungement guidance, employment barrier removal

When to Apply: After release

Eligibility: Returning citizens

Urban League of Metropolitan Chicago

Address: 4510 South Michigan Avenue, Chicago, IL 60653

Phone: (773) 285-5800

Website: www.thechicagourbanleague.org

Services Provided: Employment placement, financial literacy education, workforce training

When to Apply: After release

Eligibility: Returning citizens

State # 14: Indiana

Indiana Department of Correction – Reentry Services Division

Address: 302 West Washington Street, Indianapolis, IN 46204

Phone: (317) 232-5711

Website: www.in.gov/idoc

Services Provided: Pre-release planning, employment readiness, housing referrals, identification assistance

When to Apply: Before release and immediately after release

Eligibility: Individuals releasing from Indiana state correctional facilities

Indiana Department of Workforce Development

Address: 10 North Senate Avenue, Indianapolis, IN 46204

Phone: (317) 232-6702

Website: www.in.gov/dwd

Services Provided: Job placement, workforce training, apprenticeships, career counseling

When to Apply: Immediately after release

Eligibility: Indiana residents, including returning citizens

WorkOne Indiana Career Centers

Address: Multiple statewide locations

Phone: (800) 891-6499

Website: www.workonejobs.com

Services Provided: Employment placement, resume assistance, workforce training

When to Apply: After release

Eligibility: Returning citizens

Indiana Housing and Community Development Authority

Address: 30 South Meridian Street, Suite 900, Indianapolis, IN 46204

Phone: (317) 232-7777

Website: www.in.gov/ihcda

Services Provided: Housing assistance programs, rental support, housing referrals

When to Apply: After release

Eligibility: Returning citizens

Volunteers of America Ohio & Indiana

Address: 927 North Pennsylvania Street, Indianapolis, IN 46204

Phone: (317) 686-5800

Website: www.voaohin.org

Services Provided: Transitional housing, employment assistance, financial literacy

When to Apply: Before release and after release

Eligibility: Returning citizens

Goodwill Industries of Central & Southern Indiana

Address: 1635 West Michigan Street, Indianapolis, IN 46222

Phone: (317) 524-4313

Website: www.goodwillindy.org

Services Provided: Job training, employment placement, financial literacy education

When to Apply: After release

Eligibility: Returning citizens

Indiana Legal Services

Address: 151 North Delaware Street, Suite 1800, Indianapolis, IN 46204

Phone: (317) 631-9410

Website: www.indianalegalservices.org

Services Provided: Legal assistance, expungement guidance, employment barrier removal

When to Apply: After release

Eligibility: Returning citizens

RecycleForce

Address: 1255 Roosevelt Avenue, Indianapolis, IN 46202

Phone: (317) 532-1367

Website: www.recycleforce.org

Services Provided: Transitional employment, workforce training, financial literacy

When to Apply: After release

Eligibility: Returning citizens

PACE Indy

Address: 604 East 38th Street, Indianapolis, IN 46205

Phone: (317) 612-6800

Website: www.paceindy.org

Services Provided: Employment readiness, housing referrals, mentoring

When to Apply: Before release and after release

Eligibility: Returning citizens

Edna Martin Christian Center

Address: 2259 North Ralston Avenue, Indianapolis, IN 46218

Phone: (317) 637-3776

Website: www.ednamartincc.org

Services Provided: Employment support, financial literacy education, mentoring

When to Apply: After release

Eligibility: Returning citizens

John Boner Neighborhood Centers

Address: 2236 East 10th Street, Indianapolis, IN 46201

Phone: (317) 633-8210

Website: www.jbncenters.org

Services Provided: Employment assistance, housing support, financial education

When to Apply: After release

Eligibility: Returning citizens

Catholic Charities Indianapolis

Address: 1400 North Meridian Street, Indianapolis, IN 46202

Phone: (317) 236-1513

Website: www.archindy.org/cc

Services Provided: Housing assistance, employment support, financial counseling

When to Apply: After release

Eligibility: Returning citizens

Urban League of Indianapolis

Address: 777 Indiana Avenue, Indianapolis, IN 46202

Phone: (317) 639-5391

Website: www.indplsul.org

Services Provided: Job placement, workforce training, financial literacy education

When to Apply: After release

Eligibility: Returning citizens

Indiana Community Action Association

Address: 1845 West 18th Street, Indianapolis, IN 46202

Phone: (317) 638-4232

Website: www.incap.org

Services Provided: Housing assistance, employment support, financial literacy

When to Apply: After release

Eligibility: Returning citizens

. . .

EmployIndy

Address: 16 Tech Innovation District, Indianapolis, IN 46202

Phone: (317) 464-2024

Website: www.employindy.org

Services Provided: Job placement, workforce training, career counseling

When to Apply: After release

Eligibility: Returning citizens

Second Helpings Culinary Job Training Program

Address: 1121 Southeastern Avenue, Indianapolis, IN 46202

Phone: (317) 632-2664

Website: www.secondhelpings.org

Services Provided: Culinary job training, employment placement, workforce readiness

When to Apply: After release

Eligibility: Returning citizens

State #15: Iowa

Iowa Department of Corrections – Reentry Services Division

Address: 510 East 12th Street, Des Moines, IA 50319

Phone: (515) 725-5701

Website: www.doc.iowa.gov

Services Provided: Pre-release planning, employment readiness, housing referrals, identification assistance

When to Apply: Before release and immediately after release

Eligibility: Individuals releasing from Iowa state correctional facilities

Iowa Workforce Development

Address: 1000 East Grand Avenue, Des Moines, IA 50319

Phone: (515) 725-3665

Website: www.iowaworkforcedevelopment.gov

Services Provided: Job placement, workforce training, apprenticeships, career counseling

When to Apply: Immediately after release

Eligibility: Iowa residents, including returning citizens

IowaWORKS Career Centers

Address: Multiple statewide locations

Phone: (866) 239-0843

Website: www.iowaworks.gov

Services Provided: Employment placement, resume development, workforce readiness training

When to Apply: After release

Eligibility: Returning citizens

Iowa Department of Human Rights – Reentry Programs

Address: 321 East 12th Street, Des Moines, IA 50319

Phone: (515) 242-5655

Website: www.humanrights.iowa.gov

Services Provided: Reentry planning, employment referrals, housing assistance

When to Apply: Before release and after release

Eligibility: Returning citizens

Iowa Finance Authority

Address: 1963 Bell Avenue, Suite 200, Des Moines, IA 50315

Phone: (515) 452-0400

Website: www.iowafinance.com

Services Provided: Housing assistance programs, rental support, housing referrals

When to Apply: After release

Eligibility: Returning citizens

. . .

Urban Dreams

Address: 1615 2nd Avenue, Des Moines, IA 50314

Phone: (515) 288-4742

Website: www.urbandreams.org

Services Provided: Employment assistance, mentoring, housing referrals

When to Apply: Before release and after release

Eligibility: Returning citizens

Central Iowa Shelter & Services

Address: 1420 Mulberry Street, Des Moines, IA 50309

Phone: (515) 284-5719

Website: www.centraliowashelter.org

Services Provided: Transitional housing, employment readiness, financial education

When to Apply: After release

Eligibility: Returning citizens

The Beacon Housing Assistance

Address: 1216 East 25th Court, Des Moines, IA 50317

Phone: (515) 244-4713

Website: www.beaconiowa.org

Services Provided: Transitional housing, employment support, financial literacy

When to Apply: After release

Eligibility: Returning citizens

Primary Health Care Workforce Program

Address: 1200 University Avenue, Suite 200, Des Moines, IA 50314

Phone: (515) 248-1850

Website: www.phciowa.org

Services Provided: Employment assistance, workforce readiness, financial education

When to Apply: After release

Eligibility: Returning citizens

Iowa Center for Economic Success

Address: 2210 Grand Avenue, Des Moines, IA 50312

Phone: (515) 283-0940

Website: www.theiowacenter.org

Services Provided: Financial literacy education, credit building, employment readiness

When to Apply: After release

Eligibility: Returning citizens

Community Action Agencies of Iowa

Address: Multiple statewide locations

Phone: (515) 244-5611

Website: www.iowacommunityaction.org

Services Provided: Housing assistance, employment support, financial literacy

When to Apply: After release

Eligibility: Returning citizens

State #16: Kansas

Kansas Department of Corrections – Reentry Services Division

Address: 714 Southwest Jackson Street, Suite 300, Topeka, KS 66603

Phone: (785) 296-3317

Website: www.doc.ks.gov

Services Provided: Pre-release planning, employment readiness, housing referrals, identification assistance

When to Apply: Before release and immediately after release

Eligibility: Individuals releasing from Kansas state correctional facilities

Kansas Department of Commerce

Address: 1000 Southwest Jackson Street, Suite 100, Topeka, KS 66612

Phone: (785) 296-3481

Website: www.kansascommerce.gov

Services Provided: Job placement, workforce training, apprenticeships, career counseling

When to Apply: Immediately after release

Eligibility: Kansas residents, including returning citizens

KANSASWORKS Career Centers

Address: Multiple statewide locations

Phone: (877) 509-6757

Website: www.kansasworks.com

Services Provided: Employment placement, resume development, workforce readiness training

When to Apply: After release

Eligibility: Returning citizens

Kansas Housing Resources Corporation

Address: 611 South Kansas Avenue, Suite 300, Topeka, KS 66603

Phone: (785) 217-2001

Website: www.kshousingcorp.org

Services Provided: Housing assistance programs, rental support, housing referrals

When to Apply: After release

Eligibility: Returning citizens

Mirror, Inc.

Address: 130 East 5th Street, Newton, KS 67114
Phone: (316) 283-6740
Website: www.mirrorinc.org
Services Provided: Reentry support, employment assistance, housing referrals, mentoring
When to Apply: Before release and after release
Eligibility: Returning citizens

Catholic Charities of Northeast Kansas
Address: 9720 West 87th Street, Overland Park, KS 66212
Phone: (913) 433-2060
Website: www.catholiccharitiesks.org
Services Provided: Housing assistance, employment support, financial counseling
When to Apply: After release
Eligibility: Returning citizens

United Way of Greater Kansas City
Address: 4801 Main Street, Suite 425, Kansas City, MO 64112 (serves Kansas region)
Phone: (816) 472-4289
Website: www.unitedwaygkc.org
Services Provided: Housing referrals, employment assistance, financial literacy education
When to Apply: After release
Eligibility: Returning citizens

Urban League of Greater Kansas City
Address: 3840 Troost Avenue, Kansas City, MO 64109 (serves Kansas region)
Phone: (816) 471-0550
Website: www.ulkc.org

Services Provided: Employment placement, workforce training, financial literacy programs

When to Apply: After release

Eligibility: Returning citizens

Kansas Legal Services

Address: 712 South Kansas Avenue, Suite 200, Topeka, KS 66603

Phone: (785) 233-2068

Website: www.kansaslegalservices.org

Services Provided: Legal assistance, expungement guidance, employment barrier removal

When to Apply: After release

Eligibility: Returning citizens

Cross-Lines Community Outreach

Address: 736 Shawnee Avenue, Kansas City, KS 66105

Phone: (913) 281-3388

Website: www.cross-lines.org

Services Provided: Housing assistance, employment support, financial education

When to Apply: After release

Eligibility: Returning citizens

Salvation Army Kansas

Address: 350 North Market Street, Wichita, KS 67202

Phone: (316) 263-2769

Website: www.salvationarmykansas.org

Services Provided: Transitional housing, employment readiness, financial counseling

When to Apply: Before release and after release

Eligibility: Returning citizens

. . .

Topeka Rescue Mission

Address: 600 North Kansas Avenue, Topeka, KS 66608

Phone: (785) 354-1744

Website: www.trmonline.org

Services Provided: Transitional housing, employment readiness, financial literacy

When to Apply: After release

Eligibility: Returning citizens

State #17: Kentucky

Kentucky Department of Corrections – Reentry Services Branch

Address: 275 East Main Street, Frankfort, KY 40621

Phone: (502) 564-4726

Website: www.corrections.ky.gov

Services Provided: Pre-release planning, employment readiness, housing referrals, identification assistance

When to Apply: Before release and immediately after release

Eligibility: Individuals releasing from Kentucky state correctional facilities

Kentucky Career Center

Address: 500 Mero Street, Frankfort, KY 40601

Phone: (502) 564-7456

Website: www.kentuckycareercenter.ky.gov

Services Provided: Job placement, workforce training, apprenticeships, career counseling

When to Apply: Immediately after release

Eligibility: Kentucky residents, including returning citizens

Kentucky Career Centers (Statewide Locations)

Address: Multiple statewide locations

Phone: (800) 648-6057

Website: www.kcc.ky.gov

Services Provided: Employment placement, resume assistance, workforce readiness training

When to Apply: After release

Eligibility: Returning citizens

Kentucky Housing Corporation

Address: 1231 Louisville Road, Frankfort, KY 40601

Phone: (502) 564-7630

Website: www.kyhousing.org

Services Provided: Housing assistance programs, rental support, housing referrals

When to Apply: After release

Eligibility: Returning citizens

Goodwill Industries of Kentucky

Address: 6201 Preston Highway, Louisville, KY 40219

Phone: (502) 964-4757

Website: www.goodwillky.org

Services Provided: Job training, employment placement, financial literacy education

When to Apply: After release

Eligibility: Returning citizens

Volunteers of America Mid-States

Address: 570 South 4th Street, Suite 100, Louisville, KY 40202

Phone: (502) 636-0771

Website: www.voamid.org

Services Provided: Transitional housing, employment readiness, financial counseling

When to Apply: Before release and after release

Eligibility: Returning citizens

. . .

The Healing Place

Address: 1020 West Market Street, Louisville, KY 40202

Phone: (502) 568-6680

Website: www.thehealingplace.org

Services Provided: Transitional housing, employment readiness, life skills training

When to Apply: Before release and after release

Eligibility: Returning citizens

Catholic Charities of Louisville

Address: 435 East Broadway, Louisville, KY 40202

Phone: (502) 637-9786

Website: www.cclou.org

Services Provided: Housing assistance, employment support, financial literacy education

When to Apply: After release

Eligibility: Returning citizens

Louisville Urban League

Address: 1535 West Broadway, Louisville, KY 40203

Phone: (502) 585-4622

Website: www.lul.org

Services Provided: Employment placement, workforce training, financial literacy programs

When to Apply: After release

Eligibility: Returning citizens

Lexington Rescue Mission

Address: 444 Glen Arvin Avenue, Lexington, KY 40508

Phone: (859) 381-9600

Website: www.lexingtonrescue.org

Services Provided: Transitional housing, employment readiness, financial literacy

When to Apply: After release
Eligibility: Returning citizens

Community Action Kentucky
Address: 101 Burch Court, Frankfort, KY 40601
Phone: (502) 875-5863
Website: www.capky.org
Services Provided: Housing assistance, employment support, financial literacy education
When to Apply: After release
Eligibility: Returning citizens

Kentucky Community and Technical College System
Address: 300 North Main Street, Versailles, KY 40383
Phone: (859) 256-3100
Website: www.kctcs.edu
Services Provided: Trade certifications, workforce training, degree programs
When to Apply: After release
Eligibility: Returning citizens

Kentucky Office of Employment and Training
Address: 500 Mero Street, Frankfort, KY 40601
Phone: (502) 564-2900
Website: www.kentuckycareercenter.ky.gov
Services Provided: Job placement, workforce training, employment readiness
When to Apply: After release
Eligibility: Returning citizens

Hope Center Lexington
Address: 360 West Loudon Avenue, Lexington, KY 40508

Phone: (859) 252-7881

Website: www.hopectr.org

Services Provided: Transitional housing, employment support, financial counseling

When to Apply: After release

Eligibility: Returning citizens

State #18: Louisiana

Louisiana Department of Public Safety and Corrections – Reentry Services Division

Address: 504 Mayflower Street, Baton Rouge, LA 70802

Phone: (225) 342-6740

Website: www.doc.la.gov

Services Provided: Pre-release planning, employment readiness, housing referrals, identification assistance

When to Apply: Before release and immediately after release

Eligibility: Individuals releasing from Louisiana state correctional facilities

Louisiana Workforce Commission

Address: 1001 North 23rd Street, Baton Rouge, LA 70802

Phone: (225) 342-3111

Website: www.louisianaworks.net

Services Provided: Job placement, workforce training, apprenticeships, career counseling

When to Apply: Immediately after release

Eligibility: Louisiana residents, including returning citizens

Louisiana American Job Centers

Address: Multiple statewide locations

Phone: (866) 783-5567

Website: www.louisianaworks.net

Services Provided: Employment placement, resume assistance,

workforce readiness training

When to Apply: After release

Eligibility: Returning citizens

Louisiana Housing Corporation

Address: 2415 Quail Drive, Baton Rouge, LA 70808

Phone: (225) 763-8700

Website: www.lhc.la.gov

Services Provided: Housing assistance programs, rental support, housing referrals

When to Apply: After release

Eligibility: Returning citizens

Goodwill Industries of Southeastern Louisiana

Address: 3400 Tulane Avenue, New Orleans, LA 70119

Phone: (504) 456-2622

Website: www.goodwillno.org

Services Provided: Job training, employment placement, financial literacy education

When to Apply: After release

Eligibility: Returning citizens

Catholic Charities Archdiocese of New Orleans

Address: 1000 Howard Avenue, Suite 200, New Orleans, LA 70113

Phone: (504) 523-3755

Website: www.ccano.org

Services Provided: Housing assistance, employment support, financial literacy

When to Apply: Before release and after release

Eligibility: Returning citizens

. . .

The First 72+

Address: 2606 Saint Louis Street, New Orleans, LA 70119

Phone: (504) 399-8236

Website: www.first72plus.org

Services Provided: Reentry planning, housing assistance, employment support, mentoring

When to Apply: Before release and immediately after release

Eligibility: Returning citizens

Louisiana Center for Children's Rights Reentry Program

Address: 1100-B Milton Street, New Orleans, LA 70122

Phone: (504) 658-6860

Website: www.laccr.org

Services Provided: Employment assistance, housing referrals, mentoring

When to Apply: After release

Eligibility: Returning citizens

Urban League of Louisiana

Address: 4640 South Carrollton Avenue, New Orleans, LA 70119

Phone: (504) 620-9647

Website: www.urbanleaguela.org

Services Provided: Employment placement, workforce training, financial literacy education

When to Apply: After release

Eligibility: Returning citizens

Volunteers of America Southeast Louisiana

Address: 4152 Canal Street, New Orleans, LA 70119

Phone: (504) 482-2130

Website: www.voasela.org

Services Provided: Transitional housing, employment readiness, financial counseling

When to Apply: Before release and after release

Eligibility: Returning citizens

Southeast Louisiana Legal Services

Address: 1010 Common Street, Suite 1400, New Orleans, LA 70112

Phone: (504) 529-1000

Website: www.slls.org

Services Provided: Legal assistance, expungement guidance, employment barrier removal

When to Apply: After release

Eligibility: Returning citizens

Louisiana Community and Technical College System

Address: 265 South Foster Drive, Baton Rouge, LA 70806

Phone: (225) 922-2800

Website: www.lctcs.edu

Services Provided: Trade certifications, workforce training, degree programs

When to Apply: After release

Eligibility: Returning citizens

New Orleans Mission

Address: 1130 Oretha Castle Haley Boulevard, New Orleans, LA 70113

Phone: (504) 523-2116

Website: www.neworleansmission.org

Services Provided: Transitional housing, employment readiness, financial literacy

When to Apply: After release

Eligibility: Returning citizens

. . .

Ozanam Inn

Address: 843 Camp Street, New Orleans, LA 70130

Phone: (504) 523-1184

Website: www.ozanaminn.org

Services Provided: Transitional housing, employment support, financial counseling

When to Apply: After release

Eligibility: Returning citizens

Capital Area Human Services Reentry Program

Address: 7389 Florida Boulevard, Baton Rouge, LA 70806

Phone: (225) 922-2700

Website: www.cahsd.org

Services Provided: Reentry planning, employment assistance, mentoring

When to Apply: After release

Eligibility: Returning citizens

State #19: Maine

Maine Department of Corrections – Reentry Services Division

Address: 25 Tyson Drive, Suite 9, Augusta, ME 04330

Phone: (207) 287-2711

Website: www.maine.gov/corrections

Services Provided: Pre-release planning, employment readiness, housing referrals, identification assistance

When to Apply: Before release and immediately after release

Eligibility: Individuals releasing from Maine state correctional facilities

Maine Department of Labor

Address: 54 State House Station, Augusta, ME 04333

Phone: (207) 623-7900

Website: www.maine.gov/labor

Services Provided: Job placement, workforce training, apprenticeships, career counseling

When to Apply: Immediately after release

Eligibility: Maine residents, including returning citizens

Maine CareerCenters

Address: Multiple statewide locations

Phone: (888) 457-8883

Website: www.mainecareercenter.gov

Services Provided: Employment placement, resume assistance, workforce readiness training

When to Apply: After release

Eligibility: Returning citizens

Maine State Housing Authority

Address: 26 Edison Drive, Augusta, ME 04330

Phone: (207) 626-4600

Website: www.mainehousing.org

Services Provided: Housing assistance programs, rental support, housing referrals

When to Apply: After release

Eligibility: Returning citizens

Goodwill Northern New England

Address: 353 Cumberland Avenue, Portland, ME 04101

Phone: (207) 774-6323

Website: www.goodwillnne.org

Services Provided: Job training, employment placement, financial literacy education

When to Apply: After release

Eligibility: Returning citizens

. . .

Volunteers of America Northern New England

Address: 14 Maine Street, Brunswick, ME 04011

Phone: (207) 373-1140

Website: www.voanne.org

Services Provided: Transitional housing, employment readiness, financial counseling

When to Apply: Before release and after release

Eligibility: Returning citizens

Catholic Charities Maine

Address: 80 Sherman Street, Portland, ME 04101

Phone: (207) 523-1160

Website: www.ccmaine.org

Services Provided: Housing assistance, employment support, financial literacy education

When to Apply: After release

Eligibility: Returning citizens

Preble Street

Address: 38 Preble Street, Portland, ME 04101

Phone: (207) 775-0026

Website: www.preblestreet.org

Services Provided: Transitional housing, employment support, financial education

When to Apply: After release

Eligibility: Returning citizens

Maine Legal Services for the Elderly and Legal Aid

Address: 5 Wabanaki Way, Suite 21, Bangor, ME 04401

Phone: (207) 942-8241

Website: www.mainelse.org

Services Provided: Legal assistance, expungement guidance, employment barrier removal

When to Apply: After release
Eligibility: Returning citizens

Portland Adult Education Workforce Program
Address: 14 Locust Street, Portland, ME 04101
Phone: (207) 874-8150
Website: www.portlandadulted.org
Services Provided: Workforce training, job readiness, financial literacy education
When to Apply: After release
Eligibility: Returning citizens

Maine Community Action Partnership
Address: 155 Center Street, Suite 1, Auburn, ME 04210
Phone: (207) 626-7058
Website: www.mainecap.org
Services Provided: Housing assistance, employment support, financial literacy education
When to Apply: After release
Eligibility: Returning citizens

Fedcap Maine
Address: 5 Molly Ockett Drive, Suite 5, Fryeburg, ME 04037
Phone: (207) 935-2659
Website: www.fedcap.org
Services Provided: Employment placement, workforce training, financial literacy
When to Apply: After release
Eligibility: Returning citizens

State #20: Maryland

Maryland Department of Public Safety and Correctional Services – Reentry Services Unit

Address: 6776 Reisterstown Road, Baltimore, MD 21215

Phone: (410) 585-3300

Website: www.dpscs.maryland.gov

Services Provided: Pre-release planning, employment readiness, housing referrals, identification assistance

When to Apply: Before release and immediately after release

Eligibility: Individuals releasing from Maryland state correctional facilities

Maryland Department of Labor

Address: 1100 North Eutaw Street, Baltimore, MD 21201

Phone: (410) 767-2173

Website: www.labor.maryland.gov

Services Provided: Job placement, workforce training, apprenticeships, career counseling

When to Apply: Immediately after release

Eligibility: Maryland residents, including returning citizens

American Job Centers Maryland

Address: Multiple statewide locations

Phone: (410) 767-2173

Website: www.dllr.state.md.us/county

Services Provided: Employment placement, resume assistance, workforce readiness training

When to Apply: After release

Eligibility: Returning citizens

Maryland Department of Housing and Community Development

Address: 7800 Harkins Road, Lanham, MD 20706

Phone: (301) 429-7400

Website: www.dhcd.maryland.gov

Services Provided: Housing assistance programs, rental support, housing referrals

When to Apply: After release

Eligibility: Returning citizens

Maryland Reentry Resource Center

Address: 6776 Reisterstown Road, Baltimore, MD 21215

Phone: (410) 585-3179

Website: www.dpscs.maryland.gov

Services Provided: Reentry planning, employment referrals, housing assistance

When to Apply: Before release and after release

Eligibility: Returning citizens

Goodwill Industries of the Chesapeake

Address: 3700 Koppers Street, Baltimore, MD 21227

Phone: (410) 837-1800

Website: www.goodwillches.org

Services Provided: Job training, employment placement, financial literacy education

When to Apply: After release

Eligibility: Returning citizens

Catholic Charities of Baltimore

Address: 320 Cathedral Street, Baltimore, MD 21201

Phone: (667) 600-2000

Website: www.cc-md.org

Services Provided: Housing assistance, employment support, financial counseling

When to Apply: Before release and after release

Eligibility: Returning citizens

. . .

Vehicles for Change

Address: 4111 Washington Boulevard, Halethorpe, MD 21227

Phone: (410) 242-9674

Website: www.vehiclesforchange.org

Services Provided: Job training, employment placement, financial literacy education

When to Apply: After release

Eligibility: Returning citizens

Living Classrooms Foundation

Address: 802 South Caroline Street, Baltimore, MD 21231

Phone: (410) 685-0295

Website: www.livingclassrooms.org

Services Provided: Job training, employment assistance, workforce readiness

When to Apply: After release

Eligibility: Returning citizens

Center for Urban Families

Address: 2201 North Monroe Street, Baltimore, MD 21217

Phone: (410) 367-5691

Website: www.cfuf.org

Services Provided: Employment assistance, financial literacy education, mentoring

When to Apply: After release

Eligibility: Returning citizens

Roberta's House Reentry Support Program

Address: 928 East North Avenue, Baltimore, MD 21202

Phone: (410) 235-6633

Website: www.robertashouse.org

Services Provided: Reentry planning, employment support, mentoring

When to Apply: After release

Eligibility: Returning citizens

State #21: Massachusetts

Massachusetts Department of Correction – Reentry Services Division

Address: 50 Maple Street, Milford, MA 01757

Phone: (508) 422-3300

Website: www.mass.gov/orgs/massachusetts-department-of-correction

Services Provided: Pre-release planning, employment readiness, housing referrals, identification assistance

When to Apply: Before release and immediately after release

Eligibility: Individuals releasing from Massachusetts state correctional facilities

MassHire Department of Career Services

Address: 100 Cambridge Street, Suite 300, Boston, MA 02114

Phone: (617) 626-5300

Website: www.mass.gov/orgs/department-of-career-services

Services Provided: Job placement, workforce training, apprenticeships, career counseling

When to Apply: Immediately after release

Eligibility: Massachusetts residents, including returning citizens

MassHire Career Centers

Address: Multiple statewide locations

Phone: (617) 626-5300

Website: www.masshirema.org

Services Provided: Employment placement, resume assistance, workforce readiness training

When to Apply: After release
Eligibility: Returning citizens

Massachusetts Housing Partnership
Address: 160 Federal Street, Boston, MA 02110
Phone: (617) 330-9955
Website: www.mhp.net
Services Provided: Housing assistance programs, rental support, housing referrals
When to Apply: After release
Eligibility: Returning citizens

Goodwill Industries of Massachusetts
Address: 1010 Harrison Avenue, Boston, MA 02119
Phone: (617) 445-1010
Website: www.goodwillmass.org
Services Provided: Job training, employment placement, financial literacy education
When to Apply: After release
Eligibility: Returning citizens

SPAN (Strategic Prevention and Advocacy Network)
Address: 105 Chauncy Street, Suite 611, Boston, MA 02111
Phone: (617) 423-0750
Website: www.spanmass.org
Services Provided: Employment assistance, mentoring, housing referrals
When to Apply: Before release and after release
Eligibility: Returning citizens

Catholic Charities Boston
Address: 275 West Broadway, Boston, MA 02127

Phone: (617) 464-8500
Website: www.ccab.org
Services Provided: Housing assistance, employment support, financial literacy education
When to Apply: After release
Eligibility: Returning citizens

Community Resources for Justice
Address: 355 Boylston Street, Boston, MA 02116
Phone: (617) 482-2520
Website: www.crj.org
Services Provided: Reentry support, employment assistance, transitional housing referrals
When to Apply: Before release and after release
Eligibility: Returning citizens

Boston Reentry Initiative
Address: 1 Schroeder Plaza, Boston, MA 02120
Phone: (617) 343-4673
Website: www.boston.gov
Services Provided: Employment support, mentoring, housing referrals
When to Apply: Before release and after release
Eligibility: Returning citizens

State #22: Michigan

Michigan Department of Corrections – Offender Success Administration
Address: 206 East Michigan Avenue, Lansing, MI 48909
Phone: (517) 335-1426
Website: www.michigan.gov/corrections
Services Provided: Pre-release planning, employment readiness, housing referrals, identification assistance

When to Apply: Before release and immediately after release

Eligibility: Individuals releasing from Michigan state correctional facilities

Michigan Works!

Address: Multiple statewide locations

Phone: (800) 285-WORK

Website: www.michiganworks.org

Services Provided: Job placement, workforce training, apprenticeships, career counseling

When to Apply: Immediately after release

Eligibility: Michigan residents, including returning citizens

Michigan Department of Labor and Economic Opportunity

Address: 2407 North Grand River Avenue, Lansing, MI 48906

Phone: (517) 335-5858

Website: www.michigan.gov/leo

Services Provided: Workforce development, employment placement, career training

When to Apply: After release

Eligibility: Returning citizens

Michigan State Housing Development Authority

Address: 735 East Michigan Avenue, Lansing, MI 48912

Phone: (517) 373-8370

Website: www.michigan.gov/mshda

Services Provided: Housing assistance programs, rental support, housing referrals

When to Apply: After release

Eligibility: Returning citizens

Goodwill Industries of Greater Detroit

Address: 3111 Grand River Avenue, Detroit, MI 48208

Phone: (313) 557-4439

Website: www.goodwilldetroit.org

Services Provided: Job training, employment placement, financial literacy education

When to Apply: After release

Eligibility: Returning citizens

Detroit Reentry Center

Address: 18100 Meyers Road, Detroit, MI 48235

Phone: (313) 368-3200

Website: www.michigan.gov/corrections

Services Provided: Employment assistance, housing referrals, mentoring

When to Apply: Before release and after release

Eligibility: Returning citizens

Catholic Charities of Southeast Michigan

Address: 15945 Canal Road, Clinton Township, MI 48038

Phone: (586) 416-2300

Website: www.ccsem.org

Services Provided: Housing assistance, employment support, financial literacy education

When to Apply: After release

Eligibility: Returning citizens

Detroit Employment Solutions Corporation

Address: 440 East Congress Street, Detroit, MI 48226

Phone: (313) 876-0674

Website: www.detroitatwork.com

Services Provided: Job placement, workforce training, employment readiness

When to Apply: After release

Eligibility: Returning citizens

Nation Outside

Address: 401 South Washington Square, Lansing, MI 48933

Phone: (517) 316-4318

Website: www.nationoutside.org

Services Provided: Employment assistance, mentoring, financial literacy education

When to Apply: Before release and after release

Eligibility: Returning citizens

State #23: Minnesota

Minnesota Department of Corrections – Reentry Services Unit

Address: 1450 Energy Park Drive, Suite 200, St. Paul, MN 55108

Phone: (651) 361-7200

Website: www.mn.gov/doc

Services Provided: Pre-release planning, employment readiness, housing referrals, identification assistance

When to Apply: Before release and immediately after release

Eligibility: Individuals releasing from Minnesota state correctional facilities

Minnesota Department of Employment and Economic Development

Address: 332 Minnesota Street, Suite E200, St. Paul, MN 55101

Phone: (651) 259-7114

Website: www.mn.gov/deed

Services Provided: Job placement, workforce training, apprenticeships, career counseling

When to Apply: Immediately after release

Eligibility: Minnesota residents, including returning citizens

. . .

CareerForce Minnesota

Address: Multiple statewide locations

Phone: (651) 259-7501

Website: www.careerforcemn.com

Services Provided: Employment placement, resume development, workforce readiness training

When to Apply: After release

Eligibility: Returning citizens

Minnesota Housing Finance Agency

Address: 400 Wabasha Street North, Suite 400, St. Paul, MN 55102

Phone: (651) 296-7608

Website: www.mnhousing.gov

Services Provided: Housing assistance programs, rental support, housing referrals

When to Apply: After release

Eligibility: Returning citizens

Goodwill-Easter Seals Minnesota

Address: 553 Fairview Avenue North, St. Paul, MN 55104

Phone: (651) 379-5800

Website: www.gesmn.org

Services Provided: Job training, employment placement, financial literacy education

When to Apply: After release

Eligibility: Returning citizens

Minnesota Adult & Teen Challenge Reentry Program

Address: 1619 Portland Avenue South, Minneapolis, MN 55404

Phone: (612) 373-3366

Website: www.mntc.org

Services Provided: Transitional housing, employment readiness, mentoring

When to Apply: Before release and after release

Eligibility: Returning citizens

Better Futures Minnesota

Address: 1808 University Avenue West, Suite 300, St. Paul, MN 55104

Phone: (651) 789-7606

Website: www.betterfuturesminnesota.com

Services Provided: Employment placement, workforce training, financial literacy education

When to Apply: Before release and after release

Eligibility: Returning citizens

Urban League Twin Cities

Address: 2100 Plymouth Avenue North, Minneapolis, MN 55411

Phone: (612) 302-3100

Website: www.ultcmn.org

Services Provided: Employment placement, workforce training, financial literacy programs

When to Apply: After release

Eligibility: Returning citizens

Avivo

Address: 1900 Chicago Avenue, Minneapolis, MN 55404

Phone: (612) 752-8000

Website: www.avivomn.org

Services Provided: Job training, employment placement, financial literacy education

When to Apply: After release

Eligibility: Returning citizens

Project for Pride in Living

Address: 1035 East Franklin Avenue, Minneapolis, MN 55404
Phone: (612) 455-5100
Website: www.ppl-inc.org
Services Provided: Transitional housing, employment support, financial education
When to Apply: After release
Eligibility: Returning citizens

State #24: Mississippi

Mississippi Department of Corrections – Reentry Services Division

Address: 633 North State Street, Jackson, MS 39202
Phone: (601) 359-5600
Website: www.mdoc.ms.gov
Services Provided: Pre-release planning, employment readiness, housing referrals, identification assistance
When to Apply: Before release and immediately after release
Eligibility: Individuals releasing from Mississippi state correctional facilities

Mississippi Department of Employment Security

Address: 1235 Eastchester Drive, Jackson, MS 39211
Phone: (601) 321-6000
Website: www.mdes.ms.gov
Services Provided: Job placement, workforce training, apprenticeships, career counseling
When to Apply: Immediately after release
Eligibility: Mississippi residents, including returning citizens

WIN Job Centers Mississippi

Address: Multiple statewide locations
Phone: (601) 321-6000
Website: www.mdes.ms.gov/win-job-centers

Services Provided: Employment placement, resume assistance, workforce readiness training

When to Apply: After release

Eligibility: Returning citizens

Mississippi Home Corporation

Address: 735 Riverside Drive, Jackson, MS 39202

Phone: (601) 718-4642

Website: www.mshomecorp.com

Services Provided: Housing assistance programs, rental support, housing referrals

When to Apply: After release

Eligibility: Returning citizens

Goodwill Industries of Mississippi

Address: 1500 University Boulevard, Jackson, MS 39204

Phone: (601) 853-8111

Website: www.goodwillms.org

Services Provided: Job training, employment placement, financial literacy education

When to Apply: After release

Eligibility: Returning citizens

Catholic Charities of Jackson

Address: 850 East River Place, Jackson, MS 39202

Phone: (601) 355-8634

Website: www.catholiccharitiesjackson.org

Services Provided: Housing assistance, employment support, financial literacy

When to Apply: Before release and after release

Eligibility: Returning citizens

. . .

Mississippi Center for Reentry

Address: Jackson, MS

Phone: (601) 960-XXXX

Website: Contact local office

Services Provided: Reentry planning, employment assistance, housing referrals

When to Apply: Before release and after release

Eligibility: Returning citizens

Salvation Army Mississippi

Address: 110 Presto Lane, Jackson, MS 39206

Phone: (601) 982-4881

Website: www.salvationarmymississippi.org

Services Provided: Transitional housing, employment readiness, financial counseling

When to Apply: Before release and after release

Eligibility: Returning citizens

Mississippi Legal Services

Address: 440 North State Street, Jackson, MS 39201

Phone: (601) 948-6752

Website: www.mslegalservices.org

Services Provided: Legal assistance, expungement guidance, employment barrier removal

When to Apply: After release

Eligibility: Returning citizens

Urban League of Greater Jackson

Address: 345 McTyere Avenue, Jackson, MS 39202

Phone: (601) 353-3330

Website: www.ulgj.org

Services Provided: Employment placement, workforce training, financial literacy programs

When to Apply: After release
Eligibility: Returning citizens

Mississippi Community College Board
Address: 3825 Ridgewood Road, Jackson, MS 39211
Phone: (601) 432-6518
Website: www.mccb.edu
Services Provided: Trade certifications, workforce training, degree programs
When to Apply: After release
Eligibility: Returning citizens

Hinds Community College Workforce Development
Address: 505 East Main Street, Raymond, MS 39154
Phone: (601) 857-5261
Website: www.hindscc.edu
Services Provided: Workforce training, certifications, employment readiness
When to Apply: After release
Eligibility: Returning citizens

State #25: Missouri

Missouri Department of Corrections – Reentry Services Unit
Address: 2729 Plaza Drive, Jefferson City, MO 65109
Phone: (573) 526-6607
Website: www.doc.mo.gov
Services Provided: Pre-release planning, employment readiness, housing referrals, identification assistance
When to Apply: Before release and immediately after release
Eligibility: Individuals releasing from Missouri state correctional facilities

. . .

Missouri Job Centers

Address: Multiple statewide locations

Phone: (888) 728-5627

Website: www.jobs.mo.gov

Services Provided: Job placement, workforce training, apprenticeships, career counseling

When to Apply: Immediately after release

Eligibility: Missouri residents, including returning citizens

Missouri Department of Economic Development

Address: 301 West High Street, Jefferson City, MO 65101

Phone: (573) 751-4962

Website: www.ded.mo.gov

Services Provided: Workforce training, employment placement, career readiness programs

When to Apply: After release

Eligibility: Returning citizens

Missouri Housing Development Commission

Address: 920 Main Street, Suite 1400, Kansas City, MO 64105

Phone: (816) 759-6600

Website: www.mhdc.com

Services Provided: Housing assistance programs, rental support, housing referrals

When to Apply: After release

Eligibility: Returning citizens

Goodwill Industries of Missouri

Address: 3728 Market Street, St. Louis, MO 63110

Phone: (314) 241-3464

Website: www.mersgoodwill.org

Services Provided: Job training, employment placement, financial literacy education

When to Apply: After release
Eligibility: Returning citizens

Catholic Charities of St. Louis
Address: 4532 Lindell Boulevard, St. Louis, MO 63108
Phone: (314) 367-5500
Website: www.ccstl.org
Services Provided: Housing assistance, employment support, financial literacy education
When to Apply: Before release and after release
Eligibility: Returning citizens

Catholic Charities of Kansas City - St. Joseph
Address: 8001 Longview Road, Kansas City, MO 64134
Phone: (816) 761-1600
Website: www.catholiccharities-kcsj.org
Services Provided: Housing assistance, employment support, financial literacy education
When to Apply: After release
Eligibility: Returning citizens

Employment Connection
Address: 2838 Market Street, St. Louis, MO 63103
Phone: (314) 333-5627
Website: www.employmentstl.org
Services Provided: Job placement, workforce training, financial literacy education
When to Apply: Before release and after release
Eligibility: Returning citizens

Heartland Center for Behavioral Change
Address: 1730 Prospect Avenue, Kansas City, MO 64127

Phone: (816) 421-6670
Website: www.hccbinc.com
Services Provided: Employment readiness, housing referrals, mentoring
When to Apply: After release
Eligibility: Returning citizens

Urban League of Metropolitan St. Louis
Address: 1408 North Kingshighway Boulevard, St. Louis, MO 63113
Phone: (314) 615-3600
Website: www.ulstl.com
Services Provided: Employment placement, workforce training, financial literacy education
When to Apply: After release
Eligibility: Returning citizens

Urban League of Greater Kansas City
Address: 3840 Troost Avenue, Kansas City, MO 64109
Phone: (816) 471-0550
Website: www.ulkc.org
Services Provided: Job placement, workforce training, financial literacy education
When to Apply: After release
Eligibility: Returning citizens

Legal Services of Eastern Missouri
Address: 4232 Forest Park Avenue, St. Louis, MO 63108
Phone: (314) 534-4200
Website: www.lsem.org
Services Provided: Legal assistance, expungement guidance, employment barrier removal
When to Apply: After release

Eligibility: Returning citizens

State #26: Montana

Montana Department of Corrections – Reentry Services Division

Address: 5 South Last Chance Gulch, Helena, MT 59601

Phone: (406) 444-3930

Website: www.cor.mt.gov

Services Provided: Pre-release planning, employment readiness, housing referrals, identification assistance

When to Apply: Before release and immediately after release

Eligibility: Individuals releasing from Montana state correctional facilities

Montana Department of Labor and Industry

Address: 301 South Park Avenue, Helena, MT 59601

Phone: (406) 444-2840

Website: www.dli.mt.gov

Services Provided: Job placement, workforce training, apprenticeships, career counseling

When to Apply: Immediately after release

Eligibility: Montana residents, including returning citizens

Montana Job Service Offices

Address: Multiple statewide locations

Phone: (406) 444-2840

Website: www.jobservice.mt.gov

Services Provided: Employment placement, resume assistance, workforce readiness training

When to Apply: After release

Eligibility: Returning citizens

. . .

Montana Housing Division

Address: 301 South Park Avenue, Helena, MT 59601

Phone: (406) 841-2840

Website: www.commerce.mt.gov/housing

Services Provided: Housing assistance programs, rental support, housing referrals

When to Apply: After release

Eligibility: Returning citizens

Goodwill Industries of Northwest Montana

Address: 1600 North Avenue West, Missoula, MT 59801

Phone: (406) 541-8454

Website: www.goodwillnwmt.org

Services Provided: Job training, employment placement, financial literacy education

When to Apply: After release

Eligibility: Returning citizens

Volunteers of America Northern Rockies

Address: 1930 Grand Avenue, Billings, MT 59102

Phone: (406) 259-4868

Website: www.voanr.org

Services Provided: Transitional housing, employment readiness, financial counseling

When to Apply: Before release and after release

Eligibility: Returning citizens

Montana Legal Services Association

Address: 616 Helena Avenue, Suite 100, Helena, MT 59601

Phone: (406) 442-9830

Website: www.mtlsa.org

Services Provided: Legal assistance, expungement guidance, employment barrier removal

When to Apply: After release
Eligibility: Returning citizens

Human Resource Development Council
Address: 32 South Tracy Avenue, Bozeman, MT 59715
Phone: (406) 587-4486
Website: www.thehrdc.org
Services Provided: Housing assistance, employment support, financial literacy education
When to Apply: After release
Eligibility: Returning citizens

Montana Community Action Partnership
Address: 1717 West Main Street, Bozeman, MT 59715
Phone: (406) 587-4755
Website: www.montanacap.org
Services Provided: Housing assistance, employment support, financial literacy education
When to Apply: After release
Eligibility: Returning citizens

AWARE Inc.
Address: 501 East Lyndale Avenue, Helena, MT 59601
Phone: (406) 443-4583
Website: www.aware-inc.org
Services Provided: Employment support, housing referrals, financial education
When to Apply: After release
Eligibility: Returning citizens

United Way of Yellowstone County
Address: 2173 Overland Avenue, Billings, MT 59102

Phone: (406) 252-3839

Website: www.unitedwayyellowstone.org

Services Provided: Housing referrals, employment assistance, financial literacy education

When to Apply: After release

Eligibility: Returning citizens

Salvation Army Montana

Address: 355 South 24th Street West, Billings, MT 59102

Phone: (406) 245-7079

Website: www.salvationarmymontana.org

Services Provided: Transitional housing, employment readiness, financial counseling

When to Apply: Before release and after release

Eligibility: Returning citizens

211 Montana Reentry Support Line

Address: Statewide service

Phone: 211

Website: www.211montana.org

Services Provided: Referrals for housing, employment, financial assistance

When to Apply: Before release and after release

Eligibility: Returning citizens

State #27: Nebraska

Nebraska Department of Correctional Services – Reentry Services Division

Address: 801 West Prospector Place, Building 1, Lincoln, NE 68522

Phone: (402) 471-2654

Website: www.corrections.nebraska.gov

Services Provided: Pre-release planning, employment readiness, housing referrals, identification assistance

When to Apply: Before release and immediately after release

Eligibility: Individuals releasing from Nebraska state correctional facilities

Nebraska Department of Labor

Address: 550 South 16th Street, Lincoln, NE 68508

Phone: (402) 471-9000

Website: www.dol.nebraska.gov

Services Provided: Job placement, workforce training, apprenticeships, career counseling

When to Apply: Immediately after release

Eligibility: Nebraska residents, including returning citizens

Nebraska American Job Centers

Address: Multiple statewide locations

Phone: (402) 471-9000

Website: www.dol.nebraska.gov/EmploymentServices

Services Provided: Employment placement, resume assistance, workforce readiness training

When to Apply: After release

Eligibility: Returning citizens

Nebraska Investment Finance Authority

Address: 1230 O Street, Suite 200, Lincoln, NE 68508

Phone: (402) 434-3900

Website: www.nifa.org

Services Provided: Housing assistance programs, rental support, housing referrals

When to Apply: After release

Eligibility: Returning citizens

. . .

Goodwill Industries of Greater Nebraska

Address: 4805 North 72nd Street, Omaha, NE 68134

Phone: (402) 341-4609

Website: www.goodwillomaha.org

Services Provided: Job training, employment placement, financial literacy education

When to Apply: After release

Eligibility: Returning citizens

Catholic Charities of Omaha

Address: 5211 South 31st Street, Omaha, NE 68107

Phone: (402) 554-0520

Website: www.ccomaha.org

Services Provided: Housing assistance, employment support, financial literacy education

When to Apply: Before release and after release

Eligibility: Returning citizens

Catholic Social Services of Southern Nebraska

Address: 2241 O Street, Lincoln, NE 68510

Phone: (402) 474-1600

Website: www.cssisus.org

Services Provided: Housing assistance, employment support, financial literacy education

When to Apply: After release

Eligibility: Returning citizens

Nebraska Urban League

Address: 3040 Lake Street, Omaha, NE 68111

Phone: (402) 453-9730

Website: www.nulomaha.org

Services Provided: Job placement, workforce training, financial literacy programs

When to Apply: After release
Eligibility: Returning citizens

Center for People in Need
Address: 3901 North 27th Street, Lincoln, NE 68521
Phone: (402) 476-4357
Website: www.centerforpeople.org
Services Provided: Housing assistance, employment support, financial literacy education
When to Apply: After release
Eligibility: Returning citizens

Heartland Workforce Solutions
Address: 5752 Ames Avenue, Omaha, NE 68104
Phone: (402) 444-4700
Website: www.heartlandworks.org
Services Provided: Job placement, workforce training, employment readiness
When to Apply: After release
Eligibility: Returning citizens

State #28: Nevada

Nevada Department of Corrections – Reentry Services Division
Address: 5500 Snyder Avenue, Building 17, Carson City, NV 89701
Phone: (775) 977-5500
Website: www.doc.nv.gov
Services Provided: Pre-release planning, employment readiness, housing referrals, identification assistance
When to Apply: Before release and immediately after release
Eligibility: Individuals releasing from Nevada state correctional facilities

. . .

Nevada Department of Employment, Training and Rehabilitation

Address: 2800 East St. Louis Avenue, Las Vegas, NV 89104

Phone: (702) 486-0100

Website: www.detr.nv.gov

Services Provided: Job placement, workforce training, apprenticeships, career counseling

When to Apply: Immediately after release

Eligibility: Nevada residents, including returning citizens

Nevada JobConnect Career Centers

Address: Multiple statewide locations

Phone: (775) 684-0400

Website: www.nevadajobconnect.com

Services Provided: Employment placement, resume assistance, workforce readiness training

When to Apply: After release

Eligibility: Returning citizens

Nevada Housing Division

Address: 1830 College Parkway, Suite 200, Carson City, NV 89706

Phone: (775) 687-2240

Website: www.housing.nv.gov

Services Provided: Housing assistance programs, rental support, housing referrals

When to Apply: After release

Eligibility: Returning citizens

Goodwill of Southern Nevada

Address: 1280 West Tropical Parkway, Las Vegas, NV 89102

Phone: (702) 214-2000

Website: www.goodwillsn.org

Services Provided: Job training, employment placement, financial literacy education

When to Apply: After release

Eligibility: Returning citizens

Hope for Prisoners

Address: 3430 East Flamingo Road, Suite 350, Las Vegas, NV 89121

Phone: (702) 586-7600

Website: www.hopeforprisoners.org

Services Provided: Employment assistance, mentoring, financial literacy education

When to Apply: Before release and after release

Eligibility: Returning citizens

Catholic Charities of Southern Nevada

Address: 1501 Las Vegas Boulevard North, Las Vegas, NV 89101

Phone: (702) 385-2662

Website: www.catholiccharities.com

Services Provided: Housing assistance, employment support, financial counseling

When to Apply: After release

Eligibility: Returning citizens

Las Vegas Urban League

Address: 2470 North Decatur Boulevard, Suite 150, Las Vegas, NV 89108

Phone: (702) 636-3949

Website: www.lvul.org

Services Provided: Job placement, workforce training, financial literacy education

When to Apply: After release

Eligibility: Returning citizens

. . .

Northern Nevada HOPES

Address: 580 West 5th Street, Reno, NV 89503

Phone: (775) 786-4673

Website: www.nnhopes.org

Services Provided: Employment assistance, housing referrals, financial literacy education

When to Apply: After release

Eligibility: Returning citizens

Volunteers of America Western Region Nevada

Address: 811 East Charleston Boulevard, Las Vegas, NV 89104

Phone: (702) 385-2662

Website: www.voa.org

Services Provided: Transitional housing, employment readiness, financial counseling

When to Apply: Before release and after release

Eligibility: Returning citizens

State #29: New Hampshire

New Hampshire Department of Corrections – Reentry Services Division

Address: 105 Pleasant Street, Concord, NH 03301

Phone: (603) 271-5600

Website: www.doc.nh.gov

Services Provided: Pre-release planning, employment readiness, housing referrals, identification assistance

When to Apply: Before release and immediately after release

Eligibility: Individuals releasing from New Hampshire state correctional facilities

New Hampshire Employment Security

Address: 45 South Fruit Street, Concord, NH 03301
Phone: (603) 224-3311
Website: www.nhes.nh.gov
Services Provided: Job placement, workforce training, apprenticeships, career counseling
When to Apply: Immediately after release
Eligibility: New Hampshire residents, including returning citizens

NH Works Job Centers
Address: Multiple statewide locations
Phone: (603) 228-4100
Website: www.nhworks.org
Services Provided: Employment placement, resume assistance, workforce readiness training
When to Apply: After release
Eligibility: Returning citizens

New Hampshire Housing Finance Authority
Address: 32 Constitution Drive, Bedford, NH 03110
Phone: (603) 472-8623
Website: www.nhhfa.org
Services Provided: Housing assistance programs, rental support, housing referrals
When to Apply: After release
Eligibility: Returning citizens

Goodwill Northern New England
Address: 165 John E. Devine Drive, Manchester, NH 03103
Phone: (603) 623-5789
Website: www.goodwillnne.org
Services Provided: Job training, employment placement, financial literacy educatio
When to Apply: After release

Eligibility: Returning citizens

The Waypoint

Address: 464 Chestnut Street, Manchester, NH 03105

Phone: (603) 518-4000

Website: www.waypointnh.org

Services Provided: Employment assistance, housing referrals, financial literacy education

When to Apply: Before release and after release

Eligibility: Returning citizens

Catholic Charities New Hampshire

Address: 100 William Loeb Drive, Manchester, NH 03109

Phone: (603) 669-3030

Website: www.cc-nh.org

Services Provided: Housing assistance, employment support, financial counseling

When to Apply: After release

Eligibility: Returning citizens

Families in Transition

Address: 122 Market Street, Manchester, NH 03101

Phone: (603) 641-9441

Website: www.fitnh.org

Services Provided: Transitional housing, employment support, financial literacy education

When to Apply: After release

Eligibility: Returning citizens

New Hampshire Legal Assistance

Address: 117 North State Street, Concord, NH 03301

Phone: (603) 224-3333

Website: www.nhla.org

Services Provided: Legal assistance, expungement guidance, employment barrier removal

When to Apply: After release

Eligibility: Returning citizens

Granite United Way

Address: 22 Concord Street, Manchester, NH 03101

Phone: (603) 625-6939

Website: www.graniteuw.org

Services Provided: Housing referrals, employment assistance, financial literacy education

When to Apply: After release

Eligibility: Returning citizens

Second Start

Address: 17 Knight Street, Concord, NH 03301

Phone: (603) 228-1341

Website: www.second-start.org

Services Provided: Workforce training, employment assistance, financial literacy education

When to Apply: After release

Eligibility: Returning citizens

State #30: New Jersey

New Jersey Department of Corrections – Office of Transitional Services

Address: Whittlesey Road, Trenton, NJ 08625

Phone: (609) 292-4036

Website: www.nj.gov/corrections

Services Provided: Pre-release planning, employment readiness, housing referrals, identification assistance

When to Apply: Before release and immediately after release

Eligibility: Individuals releasing from New Jersey state correctional facilities

New Jersey Department of Labor and Workforce Development

Address: 1 John Fitch Plaza, Trenton, NJ 08611

Phone: (609) 292-2323

Website: www.nj.gov/labor

Services Provided: Job placement, workforce training, apprenticeships, career counseling

When to Apply: Immediately after release

Eligibility: New Jersey residents, including returning citizens

One-Stop Career Centers New Jersey

Address: Multiple statewide locations

Phone: (877) 872-5627

Website: www.careeronestop.org

Services Provided: Employment placement, resume assistance, workforce readiness training

When to Apply: After release

Eligibility: Returning citizens

New Jersey Housing and Mortgage Finance Agency

Address: 637 South Clinton Avenue, Trenton, NJ 08650

Phone: (609) 278-7400

Website: www.nj.gov/dca/hmfa

Services Provided: Housing assistance programs, rental support, housing referrals

When to Apply: After release

Eligibility: Returning citizens

New Jersey Reentry Corporation

Address: 591 Summit Avenue, Jersey City, NJ 07306

Phone: (201) 604-2600

Website: www.njreentry.org

Services Provided: Employment assistance, vocational training, financial literacy education

When to Apply: Before release and after release

Eligibility: Returning citizens

Goodwill Industries of Greater New York and Northern New Jersey

Address: 400 Supor Boulevard, Carlstadt, NJ 07072

Phone: (201) 933-7300

Website: www.goodwillnynj.org

Services Provided: Job training, employment placement, financial literacy education

When to Apply: After release

Eligibility: Returning citizens

Catholic Charities Diocese of Newark

Address: 590 North 7th Street, Newark, NJ 07107

Phone: (973) 596-3980

Website: www.ccannj.com

Services Provided: Housing assistance, employment support, financial counseling

When to Apply: Before release and after release

Eligibility: Returning citizens

United Way of Northern New Jersey

Address: 60 South Fullerton Avenue, Montclair, NJ 07042

Phone: (973) 993-1160

Website: www.unitedwaynnj.org

Services Provided: Housing referrals, employment assistance, financial literacy education

When to Apply: After release

Eligibility: Returning citizens

211 New Jersey Reentry Support Line

Address: Statewide service

Phone: 211

Website: www.nj211.org

Services Provided: Referrals for housing, employment, financial assistance

When to Apply: Before release and after release

Eligibility: Returning citizens

State #31: New Mexico

New Mexico Corrections Department – Reentry and Transition Services

Address: 4337 State Highway 14, Santa Fe, NM 87508

Phone: (505) 827-8700

Website: www.cd.nm.gov

Services Provided: Pre-release planning, employment readiness, housing referrals, identification assistance

When to Apply: Before release and immediately after release

Eligibility: Individuals releasing from New Mexico state correctional facilities

New Mexico Department of Workforce Solutions

Address: 401 Broadway Boulevard NE, Albuquerque, NM 87102

Phone: (505) 841-8400

Website: www.dws.state.nm.us

Services Provided: Job placement, workforce training, apprenticeships, career counseling

When to Apply: Immediately after release

Eligibility: New Mexico residents, including returning citizens

. . .

New Mexico Workforce Connection Centers

Address: Multiple statewide locations

Phone: (877) 664-6984

Website: www.jobs.state.nm.us

Services Provided: Employment placement, resume assistance, workforce readiness training

When to Apply: After release

Eligibility: Returning citizens

New Mexico Mortgage Finance Authority

Address: 344 4th Street SW, Albuquerque, NM 87102

Phone: (505) 843-6880

Website: www.housingnm.org

Services Provided: Housing assistance programs, rental support, housing referrals

When to Apply: After release

Eligibility: Returning citizens

Goodwill Industries of New Mexico

Address: 5000 San Mateo Boulevard NE, Albuquerque, NM 87109

Phone: (505) 881-6401

Website: www.goodwillnm.org

Services Provided: Job training, employment placement, financial literacy education

When to Apply: After release

Eligibility: Returning citizens

New Mexico Reentry Center

Address: Albuquerque, NM

Phone: Contact local office

Website: Contact local office

Services Provided: Reentry planning, employment assistance, housing referrals

When to Apply: Before release and after release
Eligibility: Returning citizens

Catholic Charities of Central New Mexico
Address: 2010 Bridge Boulevard SW, Albuquerque, NM 87105
Phone: (505) 724-4670
Website: www.ccasfnm.org
Services Provided: Housing assistance, employment support, financial counseling
When to Apply: After release
Eligibility: Returning citizens

Heading Home
Address: 715 Candelaria Road NE, Albuquerque, NM 87107
Phone: (505) 344-2323
Website: www.headinghome.org
Services Provided: Transitional housing, employment assistance, financial literacy
When to Apply: After release
Eligibility: Returning citizens

St. Martin's Hospitality Center
Address: 1201 3rd Street NW, Albuquerque, NM 87102
Phone: (505) 242-8578
Website: www.smhcnm.org
Services Provided: Transitional housing, employment readiness, financial counseling
When to Apply: After release
Eligibility: Returning citizens

New Mexico Legal Aid

Address: 301 Gold Avenue SW, Albuquerque, NM 87102
Phone: (505) 243-7871
Website: www.newmexicolegalaid.org
Services Provided: Legal assistance, expungement guidance, employment barrier removal
When to Apply: After release
Eligibility: Returning citizens

Urban League of Greater Southwestern New Mexico
Address: Albuquerque, NM
Phone: Contact local office
Website: Contact local office
Services Provided: Employment placement, workforce training, financial literacy education
When to Apply: After release
Eligibility: Returning citizens

State #32: New York

New York State Department of Corrections and Community Supervision – Reentry Services Division
Address: 1220 Washington Avenue, Albany, NY 12226
Phone: (518) 457-8126
Website: www.doccs.ny.gov
Services Provided: Pre-release planning, employment readiness, housing referrals, identification assistance
When to Apply: Before release and immediately after release
Eligibility: Individuals releasing from New York state correctional facilities

New York State Department of Labor
Address: State Office Campus, Building 12, Albany, NY 12240
Phone: (518) 457-9000

Website: www.labor.ny.gov

Services Provided: Job placement, workforce training, apprenticeships, career counseling

When to Apply: Immediately after release

Eligibility: New York residents, including returning citizens

New York Career Centers

Address: Multiple statewide locations

Phone: (888) 469-7365

Website: www.careeronestop.org

Services Provided: Employment placement, resume assistance, workforce readiness training

When to Apply: After release

Eligibility: Returning citizens

New York State Homes and Community Renewal

Address: 641 Lexington Avenue, New York, NY 10022

Phone: (212) 872-0400

Website: www.hcr.ny.gov

Services Provided: Housing assistance programs, rental support, housing referrals

When to Apply: After release

Eligibility: Returning citizens

The Fortune Society

Address: 29-76 Northern Boulevard, Long Island City, NY 11101

Phone: (212) 691-7554

Website: www.fortunesociety.org

Services Provided: Employment assistance, housing support, financial literacy education

When to Apply: Before release and after release

Eligibility: Returning citizens

. . .

Center for Employment Opportunities

Address: 50 Broadway, Suite 1604, New York, NY 10004

Phone: (212) 422-4430

Website: www.ceoworks.org

Services Provided: Job placement, employment readiness, financial literacy education

When to Apply: Before release and after release

Eligibility: Returning citizens

Osborne Association

Address: 809 Westchester Avenue, Bronx, NY 10455

Phone: (718) 707-2600

Website: www.osborneny.org

Services Provided: Employment assistance, housing referrals, mentoring, financial literacy

When to Apply: Before release and after release

Eligibility: Returning citizens

Goodwill Industries of Greater New York and Northern New Jersey

Address: 25 Elm Place, 5th Floor, Brooklyn, NY 11201

Phone: (718) 728-5400

Website: www.goodwillnynj.org

Services Provided: Job training, employment placement, financial literacy education

When to Apply: After release

Eligibility: Returning citizens

Catholic Charities of New York

Address: 1011 First Avenue, New York, NY 10022

Phone: (212) 371-1000

Website: www.catholiccharitiesny.org

Services Provided: Housing assistance, employment support, financial counseling

When to Apply: After release

Eligibility: Returning citizens

Urban League of Greater New York

Address: 80 Pine Street, New York, NY 10005

Phone: (212) 926-8000

Website: www.ulgny.org

Services Provided: Job placement, workforce training, financial literacy education

When to Apply: After release

Eligibility: Returning citizens

Legal Action Center

Address: 225 Varick Street, 4th Floor, New York, NY 10014

Phone: (212) 243-1313

Website: www.lac.org

Services Provided: Legal assistance, expungement guidance, employment barrier removal

When to Apply: After release

Eligibility: Returning citizens

New York Public Library Job Search Central

Address: 476 5th Avenue, New York, NY 10018

Phone: (917) 275-6975

Website: www.nypl.org

Services Provided: Employment readiness, resume assistance, financial literacy education

When to Apply: After release

Eligibility: Returning citizens

. . .

Hudson Link for Higher Education in Prison

Address: 509 West 129th Street, New York, NY 10027

Phone: (212) 865-9376

Website: www.hudsonlink.org

Services Provided: Educational programs, workforce training, employment readiness

When to Apply: Before release and after release

Eligibility: Returning citizens

The Doe Fund

Address: 232 East 84th Street, New York, NY 10028

Phone: (212) 628-5207

Website: www.doe.org

Services Provided: Employment assistance, transitional housing, financial literacy

When to Apply: Before release and after release

Eligibility: Returning citizens

State #33: North Carolina

North Carolina Department of Adult Correction – Reentry Services Division

Address: 512 North Salisbury Street, Raleigh, NC 27604

Phone: (919) 733-2126

Website: www.ncdac.gov

Services Provided: Pre-release planning, employment readiness, housing referrals, identification assistance

When to Apply: Before release and immediately after release

Eligibility: Individuals releasing from North Carolina state correctional facilities

NCWorks Career Centers

Address: Multiple statewide locations

Phone: (855) 629-6757

Website: www.ncworks.gov

Services Provided: Job placement, workforce training, apprenticeships, career counseling

When to Apply: Immediately after release

Eligibility: North Carolina residents, including returning citizens

North Carolina Department of Commerce

Address: 301 North Wilmington Street, Raleigh, NC 27601

Phone: (919) 814-4600

Website: www.commerce.nc.gov

Services Provided: Workforce training, employment placement, career readiness

When to Apply: After release

Eligibility: Returning citizens

North Carolina Housing Finance Agency

Address: 3508 Bush Street, Raleigh, NC 27609

Phone: (919) 877-5700

Website: www.nchfa.com

Services Provided: Housing assistance programs, rental support, housing referrals

When to Apply: After release

Eligibility: Returning citizens

Goodwill Industries of Central North Carolina

Address: 1235 South Eugene Street, Greensboro, NC 27406

Phone: (336) 275-9801

Website: www.goodwillnwnc.org

Services Provided: Job training, employment placement, financial literacy education

When to Apply: After release

Eligibility: Returning citizens

Center for Community Transitions

Address: 5825 Executive Center Drive, Suite 200, Charlotte, NC 28212

Phone: (704) 494-0001

Website: www.centerforcommunitytransitions.org

Services Provided: Employment assistance, housing support, financial literacy education

When to Apply: Before release and after release

Eligibility: Returning citizens

StepUp Ministry

Address: 112 South Wilmington Street, Raleigh, NC 27601

Phone: (919) 781-0156

Website: www.stepupministry.org

Services Provided: Job training, employment readiness, financial literacy education

When to Apply: After release

Eligibility: Returning citizens

Urban League of Central Carolinas

Address: 740 West 5th Street, Charlotte, NC 28202

Phone: (704) 373-2256

Website: www.urbanleaguecc.org

Services Provided: Employment placement, workforce training, financial literacy education

When to Apply: After release

Eligibility: Returning citizens

Catholic Charities Diocese of Raleigh

Address: 7200 Stonehenge Drive, Raleigh, NC 27613
Phone: (919) 821-8142
Website: www.catholiccharitiesraleigh.org
Services Provided: Housing assistance, employment support, financial counseling
When to Apply: Before release and after release
Eligibility: Returning citizens

Gissi

Address: 224 South Dawson Street, Raleigh, NC 27601
Phone: (866) 219-5262
Website: www.legalaidnc.org
Services Provided: Legal assistance, expungement guidance, employment barrier removal
When to Apply: After release
Eligibility: Returning citizens

North Carolina Community College System

Address: 200 West Jones Street, Raleigh, NC 27603
Phone: (919) 807-7100
Website: www.nccommunitycolleges.edu
Services Provided: Trade certifications, workforce training, degree programs
When to Apply: After release
Eligibility: Returning citizens

Charlotte Rescue Mission

Address: 907 West 1st Street, Charlotte, NC 28202
Phone: (704) 333-4673
Website: www.charlotterescuemission.org
Services Provided: Transitional housing, employment readiness, financial literacy education
When to Apply: After release

Eligibility: Returning citizens

State #34: North Dakota

North Dakota Department of Corrections and Rehabilitation – Reentry Services Division

Address: 3100 Railroad Avenue, Bismarck, ND 58501

Phone: (701) 328-6390

Website: www.docr.nd.gov

Services Provided: Pre-release planning, employment readiness, housing referrals, identification assistance

When to Apply: Before release and immediately after release

Eligibility: Individuals releasing from North Dakota state correctional facilities

Job Service North Dakota

Address: 1000 East Divide Avenue, Bismarck, ND 58501

Phone: (701) 328-5000

Website: www.jobsnd.com

Services Provided: Job placement, workforce training, apprenticeships, career counseling

When to Apply: Immediately after release

Eligibility: North Dakota residents, including returning citizens

North Dakota Workforce Centers

Address: Multiple statewide locations

Phone: (701) 328-5000

Website: www.jobsnd.com

Services Provided: Employment placement, resume assistance, workforce readiness training

When to Apply: After release

Eligibility: Returning citizens

. . .

North Dakota Housing Finance Agency

Address: 2624 Vermont Avenue, Bismarck, ND 58503

Phone: (701) 328-8080

Website: www.ndhfa.org

Services Provided: Housing assistance programs, rental support, housing referrals

When to Apply: After release

Eligibility: Returning citizens

Goodwill Retail Stores & Donation Centers of North Dakota

Address: 4251 17th Avenue South, Fargo, ND 58103

Phone: (701) 566-9602

Website: www.gsfymca.org (Goodwill affiliate information may vary by region)

Services Provided: Job training, employment placement, financial literacy education

When to Apply: After release

Eligibility: Returning citizens

Centre, Inc.

Address: 1237 West Divide Avenue, Bismarck, ND 58501

Phone: (701) 223-7233

Website: www.centreinc.org

Services Provided: Transitional housing, employment readiness, mentoring

When to Apply: Before release and after release

Eligibility: Returning citizens

Catholic Charities North Dakota

Address: 5201 Bishops Boulevard, Fargo, ND 58104

Phone: (701) 356-7900

Website: www.catholiccharitiesnd.org

Services Provided: Housing assistance, employment support, financial counseling

When to Apply: After release

Eligibility: Returning citizens

North Dakota Legal Services

Address: 125 Slate Drive, Suite 2, Bismarck, ND 58503

Phone: (701) 222-2110

Website: www.legalassist.org

Services Provided: Legal assistance, expungement guidance, employment barrier removal

When to Apply: After release

Eligibility: Returning citizens

Community Action Partnership North Dakota

Address: 3233 South University Drive, Fargo, ND 58104

Phone: (701) 232-2452

Website: www.capnd.org

Services Provided: Housing assistance, employment support, financial literacy education

When to Apply: After release

Eligibility: Returning citizens

North Dakota State College of Science Workforce Training

Address: 800 6th Street North, Wahpeton, ND 58076

Phone: (701) 671-2400

Website: www.ndscs.edu

Services Provided: Trade certifications, workforce training, employment readiness

When to Apply: After release

Eligibility: Returning citizens

State #35: Ohio

Ohio Department of Rehabilitation and Correction – Reentry Services Unit

Address: 4545 Fisher Road, Suite D, Columbus, OH 43228

Phone: (614) 752-1159

Website: www.drc.ohio.gov

Services Provided: Pre-release planning, employment readiness, housing referrals, identification assistance

When to Apply: Before release and immediately after release

Eligibility: Individuals releasing from Ohio state correctional facilities

Ohio Department of Job and Family Services

Address: 30 East Broad Street, Columbus, OH 43215

Phone: (614) 466-4815

Website: www.jfs.ohio.gov

Services Provided: Job placement, workforce training, apprenticeships, career counseling

When to Apply: Immediately after release

Eligibility: Ohio residents, including returning citizens

OhioMeansJobs Centers

Address: Multiple statewide locations

Phone: (888) 296-7541

Website: www.ohiomeansjobs.ohio.gov

Services Provided: Employment placement, resume assistance, workforce readiness training

When to Apply: After release

Eligibility: Returning citizens

Ohio Housing Finance Agency

Address: 2600 Corporate Exchange Drive, Columbus, OH 43231

Phone: (888) 362-6432

Website: www.ohiohome.org

Services Provided: Housing assistance programs, rental support, housing referrals

When to Apply: After release

Eligibility: Returning citizens

Alvis, Inc.

Address: 2100 Stella Court, Columbus, OH 43215

Phone: (614) 252-8402

Website: www.alvis180.org

Services Provided: Transitional housing, employment readiness, financial literacy education

When to Apply: Before release and after release

Eligibility: Returning citizens

Volunteers of America Ohio & Indiana

Address: 624 Harmon Avenue, Columbus, OH 43223

Phone: (614) 849-0145

Website: www.voaohin.org

Services Provided: Transitional housing, employment assistance, financial counseling

When to Apply: Before release and after release

Eligibility: Returning citizens

Goodwill Industries of Greater Cleveland and East Central Ohio

Address: 408 9th Street SW, Canton, OH 44707

Phone: (330) 454-9461

Website: www.goodwillgoodskills.org

Services Provided: Job training, employment placement, financial literacy education

When to Apply: After release

Eligibility: Returning citizens

. . .

Urban League of Greater Cleveland

Address: 2930 Prospect Avenue East, Cleveland, OH 44115

Phone: (216) 622-0999

Website: www.ulcleveland.org

Services Provided: Employment placement, workforce training, financial literacy education

When to Apply: After release

Eligibility: Returning citizens

Towards Employment

Address: 1255 Euclid Avenue, Suite 300, Cleveland, OH 44115

Phone: (216) 696-7310

Website: www.towardsemployment.org

Services Provided: Job placement, employment readiness, financial literacy education

When to Apply: After release

Eligibility: Returning citizens

Cincinnati Works

Address: 708 Walnut Street, Cincinnati, OH 45202

Phone: (513) 744-9675

Website: www.cincinnatiworks.org

Services Provided: Employment assistance, mentoring, financial literacy education

When to Apply: After release

Eligibility: Returning citizens

Legal Aid Society of Cleveland

Address: 1223 West 6th Street, Cleveland, OH 44113

Phone: (888) 817-3777

Website: www.lasclev.org

Services Provided: Legal assistance, expungement guidance, employment barrier removal

When to Apply: After release
Eligibility: Returning citizens

Ohio Community College System
Address: 25 South Front Street, Columbus, OH 43215
Phone: (614) 466-6000
Website: www.ohiohighered.org
Services Provided: Trade certifications, workforce training, degree programs
When to Apply: After release
Eligibility: Returning citizens

State #36: Oklahoma

Oklahoma Department of Corrections – Reentry Services Division
Address: 3400 North Martin Luther King Avenue, Oklahoma City, OK 73111
Phone: (405) 425-2500
Website: www.oklahoma.gov/doc
Services Provided: Pre-release planning, employment readiness, housing referrals, identification assistance
When to Apply: Before release and immediately after release
Eligibility: Individuals releasing from Oklahoma state correctional facilities

Oklahoma Employment Security Commission
Address: 2401 North Lincoln Boulevard, Oklahoma City, OK 73105
Phone: (405) 557-7100
Website: www.oklahoma.gov/oesc
Services Provided: Job placement, workforce training, apprenticeships, career counseling
When to Apply: Immediately after release

Eligibility: Oklahoma residents, including returning citizens

Oklahoma Works American Job Centers

Address: Multiple statewide locations

Phone: (405) 557-7100

Website: www.oklahomaworks.gov

Services Provided: Employment placement, resume assistance, workforce readiness training

When to Apply: After release

Eligibility: Returning citizens

Oklahoma Housing Finance Agency

Address: 100 Northwest 63rd Street, Suite 200, Oklahoma City, OK 73116

Phone: (405) 848-1144

Website: www.ohfa.org

Services Provided: Housing assistance programs, rental support, housing referrals

When to Apply: After release

Eligibility: Returning citizens

Center for Employment Opportunities Oklahoma

Address: Oklahoma City, OK

Phone: Contact local office

Website: www.ceoworks.org

Services Provided: Job placement, employment readiness, financial literacy education

When to Apply: Before release and after release

Eligibility: Returning citizens

Goodwill Industries of Central Oklahoma

Address: 316 South Blackwelder Avenue, Oklahoma City, OK 73108

Phone: (405) 235-4496

Website: www.okgoodwill.org

Services Provided: Job training, employment placement, financial literacy education

When to Apply: After release

Eligibility: Returning citizens

Tulsa Day Center

Address: 415 West Archer Street, Tulsa, OK 74103

Phone: (918) 583-5588

Website: www.tulsadaycenter.org

Services Provided: Housing referrals, employment assistance, financial literacy education

When to Apply: After release

Eligibility: Returning citizens

Catholic Charities of the Archdiocese of Oklahoma City

Address: 1501 North Classen Boulevard, Oklahoma City, OK 73106

Phone: (405) 523-3000

Website: www.catholiccharitiesok.org

Services Provided: Housing assistance, employment support, financial counseling

When to Apply: After release

Eligibility: Returning citizens

Urban League of Greater Oklahoma City

Address: 3900 North Martin Luther King Avenue, Oklahoma City, OK 73111

Phone: (405) 424-5243

Website: www.urbanleagueok.org

Services Provided: Job placement, workforce training, financial literacy education

When to Apply: After release

Eligibility: Returning citizens

Legal Aid Services of Oklahoma

Address: 2901 North Classen Boulevard, Suite 112, Oklahoma City, OK 73106

Phone: (405) 557-0020

Website: www.legalaidok.org

Services Provided: Legal assistance, expungement guidance, employment barrier removal

When to Apply: After release

Eligibility: Returning citizens

Oklahoma Department of Career and Technology Education

Address: 1500 West 7th Avenue, Stillwater, OK 74074

Phone: (405) 377-2000

Website: www.okcareertech.org

Services Provided: Trade certifications, workforce training, employment readiness

When to Apply: After release

Eligibility: Returning citizens

Tulsa Housing Authority

Address: 415 East Independence Street, Tulsa, OK 74106

Phone: (918) 582-0021

Website: www.tulsahousing.org

Services Provided: Housing assistance, employment referrals, financial literacy education

When to Apply: After release

Eligibility: Returning citizens

. . .

Oklahoma City Housing Authority

Address: 1700 Northeast 4th Street, Oklahoma City, OK 73117

Phone: (405) 605-3260

Website: www.ochanet.org

Services Provided: Housing assistance, employment support, financial literacy education

When to Apply: After release

Eligibility: Returning citizens

Oklahoma Department of Human Services

Address: 2400 North Lincoln Boulevard, Oklahoma City, OK 73105

Phone: (405) 522-5050

Website: www.okdhs.org

Services Provided: Financial assistance, housing support, employment referrals

When to Apply: After release

Eligibility: Returning citizens

United Way of Central Oklahoma

Address: 1444 Northwest 28th Street, Oklahoma City, OK 73106

Phone: (405) 236-8441

Website: www.unitedwayokc.org

Services Provided: Housing referrals, employment assistance, financial literacy education

When to Apply: After release

Eligibility: Returning citizens

Salvation Army Oklahoma Division

Address: 1001 North Pennsylvania Avenue, Oklahoma City, OK 73107

Phone: (405) 246-1100

Website: www.salvationarmyoklahoma.org

Services Provided: Transitional housing, employment readiness, financial counseling

When to Apply: Before release and after release

Eligibility: Returning citizens

211 Oklahoma Reentry Support Line

Address: Statewide service

Phone: 211

Website: www.211oklahoma.org

Services Provided: Referrals for housing, employment, financial assistance

When to Apply: Before release and after release

Eligibility: Returning citizens

State #37: Oregon

Oregon Department of Corrections – Reentry Services Division

Address: 3723 Fairview Industrial Drive SE, Salem, OR 97302

Phone: (503) 945-9090

Website: www.oregon.gov/doc

Services Provided: Pre-release planning, employment readiness, housing referrals, identification assistance

When to Apply: Before release and immediately after release

Eligibility: Individuals releasing from Oregon state correctional facilities

Oregon Employment Department

Address: 875 Union Street NE, Salem, OR 97311

Phone: (503) 947-1394

Website: www.oregon.gov/employ

Services Provided: Job placement, workforce training, apprenticeships, career counseling

When to Apply: Immediately after release

Eligibility: Oregon residents, including returning citizens

. . .

WorkSource Oregon Career Centers

Address: Multiple statewide locations

Phone: (503) 947-1800

Website: www.worksourceoregon.org

Services Provided: Employment placement, resume assistance, workforce readiness training

When to Apply: After release

Eligibility: Returning citizens

Oregon Housing and Community Services

Address: 725 Summer Street NE, Suite B, Salem, OR 97301

Phone: (503) 986-2000

Website: www.oregon.gov/ohcs

Services Provided: Housing assistance programs, rental support, housing referrals

When to Apply: After release

Eligibility: Returning citizens

Goodwill Industries of the Columbia Willamette

Address: 1943 Southeast 6th Avenue, Portland, OR 97214

Phone: (503) 238-6100

Website: www.meetgoodwill.org

Services Provided: Job training, employment placement, financial literacy education

When to Apply: After release

Eligibility: Returning citizens

Central City Concern

Address: 232 Northwest 6th Avenue, Portland, OR 97209

Phone: (503) 294-1681

Website: www.centralcityconcern.org

Services Provided: Transitional housing, employment assistance, financial literacy education

When to Apply: Before release and after release

Eligibility: Returning citizens

Better People

Address: Portland, OR

Phone: Contact local office

Website: www.betterpeople.org

Services Provided: Employment assistance, mentoring, housing referrals

When to Apply: Before release and after release

Eligibility: Returning citizens

Catholic Charities of Oregon

Address: 2740 Southeast Powell Boulevard, Portland, OR 97202

Phone: (503) 231-4866

Website: www.catholiccharitiesoregon.org

Services Provided: Housing assistance, employment support, financial counseling

When to Apply: After release

Eligibility: Returning citizens

Urban League of Portland

Address: 10 North Russell Street, Portland, OR 97227

Phone: (503) 280-2600

Website: www.ulpdx.org

Services Provided: Employment placement, workforce training, financial literacy education

When to Apply: After release

Eligibility: Returning citizens

. . .

Oregon Law Center

Address: 522 Southwest 5th Avenue, Suite 812, Portland, OR 97204

Phone: (503) 473-8329

Website: www.oregonlawcenter.org

Services Provided: Legal assistance, expungement guidance, employment barrier removal

When to Apply: After release

Eligibility: Returning citizens

Portland Community College Workforce Training

Address: 12000 Southwest 49th Avenue, Portland, OR 97219

Phone: (971) 722-6111

Website: www.pcc.edu

Services Provided: Trade certifications, workforce training, employment readiness

When to Apply: After release

Eligibility: Returning citizens

Transition Projects

Address: 650 Northwest Irving Street, Portland, OR 97209

Phone: (503) 280-4700

Website: www.tprojects.org

Services Provided: Transitional housing, employment readiness, financial literacy education

When to Apply: After release

Eligibility: Returning citizens

State #38: Pennsylvania

Pennsylvania Department of Corrections – Reentry Services Division

Address: 1920 Technology Parkway, Mechanicsburg, PA 17050

Phone: (717) 728-2573

Website: www.cor.pa.gov

Services Provided: Pre-release planning, employment readiness, housing referrals, identification assistance

When to Apply: Before release and immediately after release

Eligibility: Individuals releasing from Pennsylvania state correctional facilities

Pennsylvania Department of Labor and Industry

Address: 651 Boas Street, Harrisburg, PA 17121

Phone: (717) 787-7530

Website: www.dli.pa.gov

Services Provided: Job placement, workforce training, apprenticeships, career counseling

When to Apply: Immediately after release

Eligibility: Pennsylvania residents, including returning citizens

PA CareerLink Career Centers

Address: Multiple statewide locations

Phone: (833) 750-5627

Website: www.pacareerlink.pa.gov

Services Provided: Employment placement, resume assistance, workforce readiness training

When to Apply: After release

Eligibility: Returning citizens

Pennsylvania Housing Finance Agency

Address: 211 North Front Street, Harrisburg, PA 17101

Phone: (717) 780-3800

Website: www.phfa.org

Services Provided: Housing assistance programs, rental support, housing referrals

When to Apply: After release

Eligibility: Returning citizens

. . .

Pennsylvania Prison Society

Address: 230 South Broad Street, Suite 605, Philadelphia, PA 19102

Phone: (215) 564-4775

Website: www.prisonsociety.org

Services Provided: Employment assistance, reentry planning, mentoring, financial literacy

When to Apply: Before release and after release

Eligibility: Returning citizens

Center for Employment Opportunities Pennsylvania

Address: Philadelphia, PA

Phone: Contact local office

Website: www.ceoworks.org

Services Provided: Job placement, employment readiness, financial literacy education

When to Apply: Before release and after release

Eligibility: Returning citizens

Goodwill Industries of Southeastern Pennsylvania

Address: 118 52nd Street, Philadelphia, PA 19139

Phone: (215) 879-7700

Website: www.goodwillsew.com

Services Provided: Job training, employment placement, financial literacy education

When to Apply: After release

Eligibility: Returning citizens

Urban League of Greater Philadelphia

Address: 121 South Broad Street, Philadelphia, PA 19107

Phone: (215) 985-3220

Website: www.urbanleaguephila.org

Services Provided: Employment placement, workforce training, financial literacy education

When to Apply: After release

Eligibility: Returning citizens

Catholic Charities of the Archdiocese of Philadelphia

Address: 222 North 17th Street, Philadelphia, PA 19103

Phone: (215) 587-3500

Website: www.catholiccharitiesphila.org

Services Provided: Housing assistance, employment support, financial counseling

When to Apply: Before release and after release

Eligibility: Returning citizens

Volunteers of America Pennsylvania

Address: 2112 Walnut Street, Harrisburg, PA 17103

Phone: (717) 236-1440

Website: www.voapa.org

Services Provided: Transitional housing, employment readiness, financial literacy education

When to Apply: Before release and after release

Eligibility: Returning citizens

State #39: Rhode Island

Rhode Island Department of Corrections – Reentry Services Division

Address: 40 Howard Avenue, Cranston, RI 02920

Phone: (401) 462-1000

Website: www.doc.ri.gov

Services Provided: Pre-release planning, employment readiness, housing referrals, identification assistance

When to Apply: Before release and immediately after release

Eligibility: Individuals releasing from Rhode Island state correctional facilities

Rhode Island Department of Labor and Training

Address: 1511 Pontiac Avenue, Cranston, RI 02920

Phone: (401) 462-8000

Website: www.dlt.ri.gov

Services Provided: Job placement, workforce training, apprenticeships, career counseling

When to Apply: Immediately after release

Eligibility: Rhode Island residents, including returning citizens

Rhode Island American Job Centers

Address: Multiple statewide locations

Phone: (401) 462-8800

Website: www.dlt.ri.gov/jobseekers

Services Provided: Employment placement, resume assistance, workforce readiness training

When to Apply: After release

Eligibility: Returning citizens

Rhode Island Housing

Address: 44 Washington Street, Providence, RI 02903

Phone: (401) 457-1234

Website: www.rihousing.com

Services Provided: Housing assistance programs, rental support, housing referrals

When to Apply: After release

Eligibility: Returning citizens

Amos House

Address: 460 Pine Street, Providence, RI 02907

Phone: (401) 421-7272

Website: www.amoshouse.com

Services Provided: Transitional housing, employment assistance, financial literacy education

When to Apply: Before release and after release

Eligibility: Returning citizens

Crossroads Rhode Island

Address: 160 Broad Street, Providence, RI 02903

Phone: (401) 521-2255

Website: www.crossroadsri.org

Services Provided: Transitional housing, employment readiness, financial literacy education

When to Apply: After release

Eligibility: Returning citizens

Goodwill Industries of Rhode Island

Address: 100 Houghton Street, Providence, RI 02904

Phone: (401) 861-2080

Website: www.goodwillri.org

Services Provided: Job training, employment placement, financial literacy education

When to Apply: After release

Eligibility: Returning citizens

Urban League of Rhode Island

Address: 246 Prairie Avenue, Providence, RI 02905

Phone: (401) 351-5000

Website: www.ulri.org

Services Provided: Employment placement, workforce training, financial literacy education

When to Apply: After release

Eligibility: Returning citizens

. . .

Catholic Social Services of Rhode Island

Address: 80 Broad Street, Providence, RI 02903

Phone: (401) 278-4500

Website: www.dioceseofprovidence.org

Services Provided: Housing assistance, employment support, financial counseling

When to Apply: After release

Eligibility: Returning citizens

Rhode Island Legal Services

Address: 56 Pine Street, Suite 400, Providence, RI 02903

Phone: (401) 274-2652

Website: www.rils.org

Services Provided: Legal assistance, expungement guidance, employment barrier removal

When to Apply: After release

Eligibility: Returning citizens

State #40: South Carolina

South Carolina Department of Corrections – Reentry Services Division

Address: 4444 Broad River Road, Columbia, SC 29210

Phone: (803) 896-8500

Website: www.doc.sc.gov

Services Provided: Pre-release planning, employment readiness, housing referrals, identification assistance

When to Apply: Before release and immediately after release

Eligibility: Individuals releasing from South Carolina state correctional facilities

South Carolina Department of Employment and Workforce

Address: 1550 Gadsden Street, Columbia, SC 29201
Phone: (803) 737-2400
Website: www.dew.sc.gov
Services Provided: Job placement, workforce training, apprenticeships, career counseling
When to Apply: Immediately after release
Eligibility: South Carolina residents, including returning citizens

SC Works Centers
Address: Multiple statewide locations
Phone: (800) 285-9950
Website: www.scworks.org
Services Provided: Employment placement, resume assistance, workforce readiness training
When to Apply: After release
Eligibility: Returning citizens

State #41: South Dakota

South Dakota Department of Corrections – Reentry Services Division
Address: 3200 East Highway 34, Pierre, SD 57501
Phone: (605) 773-3478
Website: www.doc.sd.gov
Services Provided: Pre-release planning, employment readiness, housing referrals, identification assistance
When to Apply: Before release and immediately after release
Eligibility: Individuals releasing from South Dakota state correctional facilities

South Dakota Department of Labor and Regulation
Address: 420 South Roosevelt Street, Aberdeen, SD 57401
Phone: (605) 626-2314
Website: www.dlr.sd.gov

Services Provided: Job placement, workforce training, apprenticeships, career counseling

When to Apply: Immediately after release

Eligibility: South Dakota residents, including returning citizens

South Dakota Job Service Offices

Address: Multiple statewide locations

Phone: (605) 626-2314

Website: www.sdjobs.org

Services Provided: Employment placement, resume assistance, workforce readiness training

When to Apply: After release

Eligibility: Returning citizens

South Dakota Housing Development Authority

Address: 3060 East Elizabeth Street, Pierre, SD 57501

Phone: (605) 773-3181

Website: www.sdhda.org

Services Provided: Housing assistance programs, rental support, housing referrals

When to Apply: After release

Eligibility: Returning citizens

Volunteers of America Dakotas

Address: 1300 West Russell Street, Sioux Falls, SD 57104

Phone: (605) 334-1414

Website: www.voa-dakotas.org

Services Provided: Transitional housing, employment assistance, financial literacy education

When to Apply: Before release and after release

Eligibility: Returning citizens

. . .

Goodwill of the Great Plains

Address: 3100 West 41st Street, Sioux Falls, SD 57105

Phone: (605) 357-6161

Website: www.goodwillgreatplains.org

Services Provided: Job training, employment placement, financial literacy education

When to Apply: After release

Eligibility: Returning citizens

Cornerstone Rescue Mission

Address: 30 Main Street, Rapid City, SD 57701

Phone: (605) 341-2844

Website: www.cornerstonemission.org

Services Provided: Transitional housing, employment readiness, financial literacy education

When to Apply: After release

Eligibility: Returning citizens

Lutheran Social Services of South Dakota

Address: 705 East 41st Street, Suite 200, Sioux Falls, SD 57105

Phone: (605) 444-7800

Website: www.lsssd.org

Services Provided: Housing assistance, employment support, financial counseling

When to Apply: After release

Eligibility: Returning citizens

South Dakota Legal Services

Address: 335 North Main Avenue, Suite 200, Sioux Falls, SD 57104

Phone: (605) 336-9230

Website: www.sdlegalaid.org

Services Provided: Legal assistance, expungement guidance, employment barrier removal

When to Apply: After release

Eligibility: Returning citizens

South Dakota Technical College System

Address: Multiple statewide locations

Phone: (605) 773-3134

Website: www.sdbor.edu

Services Provided: Trade certifications, workforce training, employment readiness

When to Apply: After release

Eligibility: Returning citizens

211 South Dakota Reentry Support Line

Address: Statewide service

Phone: 211

Website: www.helplinecenter.org/211

Services Provided: Referrals for housing, employment, financial assistance

When to Apply: Before release and after release

Eligibility: Returning citizens

State #42: Tennessee

Tennessee Department of Correction – Reentry Services Division

Address: 320 Sixth Avenue North, Nashville, TN 37243

Phone: (615) 741-1000

Website: www.tn.gov/correction

Services Provided: Pre-release planning, employment readiness, housing referrals, identification assistance

When to Apply: Before release and immediately after release

Eligibility: Individuals releasing from Tennessee state correctional facilities

Tennessee Department of Labor and Workforce Development

Address: 220 French Landing Drive, Nashville, TN 37243

Phone: (844) 224-5818

Website: www.tn.gov/workforce

Services Provided: Job placement, workforce training, apprenticeships, career counseling

When to Apply: Immediately after release

Eligibility: Tennessee residents, including returning citizens

American Job Centers of Tennessee

Address: Multiple statewide locations

Phone: (844) 224-5818

Website: www.jobs4tn.gov

Services Provided: Employment placement, resume assistance, workforce readiness training

When to Apply: After release

Eligibility: Returning citizens

Tennessee Housing Development Agency

Address: 502 Deaderick Street, Nashville, TN 37243

Phone: (615) 815-2200

Website: www.thda.org

Services Provided: Housing assistance programs, rental support, housing referrals

When to Apply: After release

Eligibility: Returning citizens

Tennessee Reentry Collaborative

Address: Nashville, TN

Phone: Contact local office

Website: www.tnreentrycollaborative.org

Services Provided: Employment assistance, mentoring, housing referrals

When to Apply: Before release and after release

Eligibility: Returning citizens

Center for Employment Opportunities Tennessee

Address: Nashville, TN

Phone: Contact local office

Website: www.ceoworks.org

Services Provided: Job placement, employment readiness, financial literacy education

When to Apply: Before release and after release

Eligibility: Returning citizens

Goodwill Industries of Middle Tennessee

Address: 937 Herman Street, Nashville, TN 37208

Phone: (615) 742-4151

Website: www.giveit2goodwill.org

Services Provided: Job training, employment placement, financial literacy education

When to Apply: After release

Eligibility: Returning citizens

Operation Stand Down Tennessee

Address: 1125 12th Avenue South, Nashville, TN 37203

Phone: (615) 248-1981

Website: www.osdtn.org

Services Provided: Employment assistance, housing referrals, financial literacy education

When to Apply: After release

Eligibility: Returning citizens

. . .

Urban League of Middle Tennessee

Address: 15 Jefferson Street, Nashville, TN 37208

Phone: (615) 254-0525

Website: www.ulmt.org

Services Provided: Job placement, workforce training, financial literacy education

When to Apply: After release

Eligibility: Returning citizens

Catholic Charities of Tennessee

Address: 2806 McGavock Pike, Nashville, TN 37214

Phone: (615) 352-3087

Website: www.cctenn.org

Services Provided: Housing assistance, employment support, financial counseling

When to Apply: After release

Eligibility: Returning citizens

Legal Aid Society of Middle Tennessee and the Cumberlands

Address: 1321 Murfreesboro Pike, Suite 400, Nashville, TN 37217

Phone: (800) 238-1443

Website: www.las.org

Services Provided: Legal assistance, expungement guidance, employment barrier removal

When to Apply: After release

Eligibility: Returning citizens

Tennessee College of Applied Technology

Address: Multiple statewide locations

Phone: (615) 366-4400

Website: www.tcat.edu

Services Provided: Trade certifications, workforce training, employment readiness

When to Apply: After release

Eligibility: Returning citizens

Nashville Rescue Mission

Address: 639 Lafayette Street, Nashville, TN 37203

Phone: (615) 255-2475

Website: www.nashvillerescuemission.org

Services Provided: Transitional housing, employment readiness, financial literacy education

When to Apply: After release

Eligibility: Returning citizens

<u>**State #43: Texas**</u>

Texas Department of Criminal Justice – Reentry and Integration Division

Address: 209 West 14th Street, Austin, TX 78701

Phone: (936) 437-2101

Website: www.tdcj.texas.gov

Services Provided: Pre-release planning, employment readiness, housing referrals, identification assistance

When to Apply: Before release and immediately after release

Eligibility: Individuals releasing from Texas state correctional facilities

Texas Workforce Commission

Address: 101 East 15th Street, Austin, TX 78778

Phone: (800) 628-5115

Website: www.twc.texas.gov

Services Provided: Job placement, workforce training, apprenticeships, career counseling

When to Apply: Immediately after release

Eligibility: Texas residents, including returning citizens

Workforce Solutions Texas Career Centers

Address: Multiple statewide locations

Phone: (800) 628-5115

Website: www.workforcesolutions.net

Services Provided: Employment placement, resume assistance, workforce readiness training

When to Apply: After release

Eligibility: Returning citizens

Texas Department of Housing and Community Affairs

Address: 221 East 11th Street, Austin, TX 78701

Phone: (800) 525-0657

Website: www.tdhca.texas.gov

Services Provided: Housing assistance programs, rental support, housing referrals

When to Apply: After release

Eligibility: Returning citizens

Texas Offenders Reentry Initiative

Address: Houston, TX

Phone: Contact local office

Website: www.texasreentry.org

Services Provided: Employment assistance, mentoring, housing referrals

When to Apply: Before release and after release

Eligibility: Returning citizens

Goodwill Industries of Central Texas

Address: 1015 Norwood Park Boulevard, Austin, TX 78753

Phone: (512) 637-7100

Website: www.goodwillcentraltexas.org

Services Provided: Job training, employment placement, financial literacy education

When to Apply: After release

Eligibility: Returning citizens

The Fortune Society Texas Programs

Address: Dallas, TX

Phone: Contact local office

Website: www.fortunesociety.org

Services Provided: Employment assistance, mentoring, financial literacy education

When to Apply: Before release and after release

Eligibility: Returning citizens

Catholic Charities of Texas

Address: Multiple statewide locations

Phone: (512) 651-6100

Website: www.catholiccharitiesusa.org

Services Provided: Housing assistance, employment support, financial counseling

When to Apply: After release

Eligibility: Returning citizens

Urban League of Greater Dallas

Address: 4315 South Lancaster Road, Dallas, TX 75216

Phone: (214) 915-4600

Website: www.ulgdallas.org

Services Provided: Job placement, workforce training, financial literacy education

When to Apply: After release

Eligibility: Returning citizens

. . .

Dallas Housing Authority

Address: 3939 North Hampton Road, Dallas, TX 75212

Phone: (214) 951-8300

Website: www.dhadal.com

Services Provided: Housing assistance, employment referrals, financial literacy education

When to Apply: After release

Eligibility: Returning citizens

Texas Health and Human Services

Address: 4900 North Lamar Boulevard, Austin, TX 78751

Phone: (512) 424-6500

Website: www.hhs.texas.gov

Services Provided: Financial assistance, housing support, employment referrals

When to Apply: After release

Eligibility: Returning citizens

United Way of Texas

Address: Multiple statewide locations

Phone: (512) 472-6267

Website: www.unitedwaytexas.org

Services Provided: Housing referrals, employment assistance, financial literacy education

When to Apply: After release

Eligibility: Returning citizens

Salvation Army Texas Division

Address: 1500 Austin Street, Houston, TX 77002

Phone: (713) 650-6530

Website: www.salvationarmytexas.org

Services Provided: Transitional housing, employment readiness, financial counseling

When to Apply: Before release and after release

Eligibility: Returning citizens

211 Texas Reentry Support Line

Address: Statewide service

Phone: 211

Website: www.211texas.org

Services Provided: Referrals for housing, employment, financial assistance

When to Apply: Before release and after release

Eligibility: Returning citizens

State #44: Utah

Utah Department of Corrections – Reentry and Rehabilitation Division

Address: 14717 South Minuteman Drive, Draper, UT 84020

Phone: (801) 545-5500

Website: www.corrections.utah.gov

Services Provided: Pre-release planning, employment readiness, housing referrals, identification assistance

When to Apply: Before release and immediately after release

Eligibility: Individuals releasing from Utah state correctional facilities

Utah Department of Workforce Services

Address: 140 East 300 South, Salt Lake City, UT 84111

Phone: (801) 526-9235

Website: www.jobs.utah.gov

Services Provided: Job placement, workforce training, apprenticeships, career counseling

When to Apply: Immediately after release

Eligibility: Utah residents, including returning citizens

. . .

Utah Employment Centers

Address: Multiple statewide locations

Phone: (801) 526-9235

Website: www.jobs.utah.gov

Services Provided: Employment placement, resume assistance, workforce readiness training

When to Apply: After release

Eligibility: Returning citizens

Utah Housing Corporation

Address: 2479 South Lake Park Boulevard, West Valley City, UT 84120

Phone: (801) 902-8200

Website: www.utahhousingcorp.org

Services Provided: Housing assistance programs, rental support, housing referrals

When to Apply: After release

Eligibility: Returning citizens

The Other Side Academy

Address: 667 East 100 South, Salt Lake City, UT 84102

Phone: (801) 953-0404

Website: www.theothersideacademy.com

Services Provided: Transitional housing, employment training, financial literacy education

When to Apply: Before release and after release

Eligibility: Returning citizens

Goodwill Industries of Utah

Address: 1625 Wall Avenue, Ogden, UT 84404

Phone: (801) 627-1658

Website: www.goodwillutah.org

Services Provided: Job training, employment placement, financial literacy education

When to Apply: After release

Eligibility: Returning citizens

Utah Community Action

Address: 815 South Freedom Boulevard, Provo, UT 84601

Phone: (801) 691-5200

Website: www.utahca.org

Services Provided: Housing assistance, employment support, financial literacy education

When to Apply: After release

Eligibility: Returning citizens

Catholic Community Services of Utah

Address: 224 North 2200 West, Salt Lake City, UT 84116

Phone: (801) 977-9119

Website: www.ccsutah.org

Services Provided: Housing assistance, employment support, financial counseling

When to Apply: After release

Eligibility: Returning citizens

Urban League of Utah

Address: 999 South Main Street, Salt Lake City, UT 84111

Phone: (801) 581-8066

Website: www.urbanleagueutah.org

Services Provided: Employment placement, workforce training, financial literacy education

When to Apply: After release

Eligibility: Returning citizens

State #45: Vermont

Vermont Department of Corrections – Reentry Services Division

Address: 280 State Drive, Waterbury, VT 05671

Phone: (802) 241-2442

Website: www.doc.vermont.gov

Services Provided: Pre-release planning, employment readiness, housing referrals, identification assistance

When to Apply: Before release and immediately after release

Eligibility: Individuals releasing from Vermont state correctional facilities

Vermont Department of Labor

Address: 5 Green Mountain Drive, Montpelier, VT 05601

Phone: (802) 828-4000

Website: www.labor.vermont.gov

Services Provided: Job placement, workforce training, apprenticeships, career counseling

When to Apply: Immediately after release

Eligibility: Vermont residents, including returning citizens

Vermont JobLink Career Centers

Address: Multiple statewide locations

Phone: (802) 828-4000

Website: www.vtlmi.info

Services Provided: Employment placement, resume assistance, workforce readiness training

When to Apply: After release

Eligibility: Returning citizens

Vermont Housing Finance Agency

Address: 164 Saint Paul Street, Burlington, VT 05401

Phone: (802) 864-5743

Website: www.vhfa.org

Services Provided: Housing assistance programs, rental support, housing referrals

When to Apply: After release

Eligibility: Returning citizens

Goodwill Industries of Northern New England

Address: 21 Dorset Lane, Williston, VT 05495

Phone: (802) 879-0088

Website: www.goodwillnne.org

Services Provided: Job training, employment placement, financial literacy education

When to Apply: After release

Eligibility: Returning citizens

Vermont Reentry Initiative

Address: Burlington, VT

Phone: Contact local office

Website: www.vermontreentry.org

Services Provided: Employment assistance, mentoring, housing referrals

When to Apply: Before release and after release

Eligibility: Returning citizens

Champlain Housing Trust

Address: 88 King Street, Burlington, VT 05401

Phone: (802) 862-6244

Website: www.getahome.org

Services Provided: Housing assistance, employment support, financial literacy education

When to Apply: After release

Eligibility: Returning citizens

. . .

COTS (Committee on Temporary Shelter)

Address: 95 North Avenue, Burlington, VT 05401

Phone: (802) 864-7402

Website: www.cotsonline.org

Services Provided: Transitional housing, employment readiness, financial literacy education

When to Apply: After release

Eligibility: Returning citizens

Catholic Charities of Vermont

Address: 55 Joy Drive, South Burlington, VT 05403

Phone: (802) 658-6110

Website: www.vermontcatholic.org

Services Provided: Housing assistance, employment support, financial counseling

When to Apply: After release

Eligibility: Returning citizens

State #46: Virginia

Virginia Department of Corrections – Reentry and Programs Division

Address: 6900 Atmore Drive, Richmond, VA 23225

Phone: (804) 674-3000

Website: www.vadoc.virginia.gov

Services Provided: Pre-release planning, employment readiness, housing referrals, identification assistance

When to Apply: Before release and immediately after release

Eligibility: Individuals releasing from Virginia state correctional facilities

Virginia Employment Commission

Address: 703 East Main Street, Richmond, VA 23219

Phone: (866) 832-2363

Website: www.vec.virginia.gov

Services Provided: Job placement, workforce training, apprenticeships, career counseling

When to Apply: Immediately after release

Eligibility: Virginia residents, including returning citizens

Virginia Career Works Centers

Address: Multiple statewide locations

Phone: (866) 832-2363

Website: www.virginiacareerworks.com

Services Provided: Employment placement, resume assistance, workforce readiness training

When to Apply: After release

Eligibility: Returning citizens

Virginia Housing

Address: 601 South Belvidere Street, Richmond, VA 23220

Phone: (804) 782-1986

Website: www.virginiahousing.com

Services Provided: Housing assistance programs, rental support, housing referrals

When to Apply: After release

Eligibility: Returning citizens

Virginia CARES

Address: 10700 Midlothian Turnpike, Suite 200, Richmond, VA 23235

Phone: (804) 643-2746

Website: www.vacares.org

Services Provided: Employment assistance, housing referrals, financial literacy education

When to Apply: Before release and after release

Eligibility: Returning citizens

. . .

Goodwill Industries of the Valleys

Address: 2502 Melrose Avenue NW, Roanoke, VA 24017

Phone: (540) 581-0620

Website: www.goodwillvalleys.com

Services Provided: Job training, employment placement, financial literacy education

When to Apply: After release

Eligibility: Returning citizens

OAR (Opportunities, Alternatives, and Resources)

Address: 10640 Page Avenue, Suite 300, Fairfax, VA 22030

Phone: (703) 246-3033

Website: www.oaronline.org

Services Provided: Employment assistance, mentoring, housing referrals

When to Apply: Before release and after release

Eligibility: Returning citizens

Catholic Charities of Eastern Virginia

Address: 5361-A Virginia Beach Boulevard, Virginia Beach, VA 23462

Phone: (757) 456-2366

Website: www.cceva.org

Services Provided: Housing assistance, employment support, financial counseling

When to Apply: After release

Eligibility: Returning citizens

Urban League of Hampton Roads

Address: 7300 Newport Avenue, Suite 500, Norfolk, VA 23505

Phone: (757) 627-0864

Website: www.ulhr.org

Services Provided: Job placement, workforce training, financial literacy education

When to Apply: After release

Eligibility: Returning citizens

Legal Aid Justice Center

Address: 123 East Broad Street, Richmond, VA 23219

Phone: (804) 643-1086

Website: www.justice4all.org

Services Provided: Legal assistance, expungement guidance, employment barrier removal

When to Apply: After release

Eligibility: Returning citizens

Virginia Community College System Workforce Programs

Address: 101 North 14th Street, Richmond, VA 23219

Phone: (804) 819-4900

Website: www.vccs.edu

Services Provided: Trade certifications, workforce training, employment readiness

When to Apply: After release

Eligibility: Returning citizens

Richmond Redevelopment and Housing Authority

Address: 901 Chamberlayne Parkway, Richmond, VA 23220

Phone: (804) 780-4200

Website: www.rrha.com

Services Provided: Housing assistance, employment support, financial literacy education

When to Apply: After release

Eligibility: Returning citizens

. . .

Norfolk Redevelopment and Housing Authority

Address: 555 East Main Street, Norfolk, VA 23510

Phone: (757) 623-1111

Website: www.nrha.us

Services Provided: Housing assistance, employment referrals, financial literacy education

When to Apply: After release

Eligibility: Returning citizens

Virginia Department of Social Services

Address: 801 East Main Street, Richmond, VA 23219

Phone: (804) 726-7000

Website: www.dss.virginia.gov

Services Provided: Financial assistance, housing support, employment referrals

When to Apply: After release

Eligibility: Returning citizens

United Way of Virginia

Address: Multiple statewide locations

Phone: (804) 330-7400

Website: www.unitedway.org/local/united-states/virginia

Services Provided: Housing referrals, employment assistance, financial literacy education

When to Apply: After release

Eligibility: Returning citizens

Salvation Army Virginia Division

Address: 2 West Grace Street, Richmond, VA 23220

Phone: (804) 225-7470

Website: www.salvationarmypotomac.org

Services Provided: Transitional housing, employment readiness, financial counseling

When to Apply: Before release and after release
Eligibility: Returning citizens

211 Virginia Reentry Support Line
Address: Statewide service
Phone: 211
Website: www.211virginia.org
Services Provided: Referrals for housing, employment, financial assistance
When to Apply: Before release and after release
Eligibility: Returning citizens

State #47: Washington

Washington State Department of Corrections – Reentry Division
Address: 7345 Linderson Way SW, Tumwater, WA 98501
Phone: (360) 725-8213
Website: www.doc.wa.gov
Services Provided: Pre-release planning, employment readiness, housing referrals, identification assistance
When to Apply: Before release and immediately after release
Eligibility: Individuals releasing from Washington state correctional facilities

Washington State Employment Security Department
Address: 212 Maple Park Avenue SE, Olympia, WA 98501
Phone: (360) 902-9500
Website: www.esd.wa.gov
Services Provided: Job placement, workforce training, apprenticeships, career counseling
When to Apply: Immediately after release
Eligibility: Washington residents, including returning citizens

. . .

WorkSource Washington Centers

Address: Multiple statewide locations

Phone: (800) 562-2308

Website: www.worksourcewa.com

Services Provided: Employment placement, resume assistance, workforce readiness training

When to Apply: After release

Eligibility: Returning citizens

Washington State Housing Finance Commission

Address: 1000 2nd Avenue, Suite 2700, Seattle, WA 98104

Phone: (206) 464-7139

Website: www.wshfc.org

Services Provided: Housing assistance programs, rental support, housing referrals

When to Apply: After release

Eligibility: Returning citizens

Pioneer Human Services

Address: 7440 West Marginal Way South, Seattle, WA 98108

Phone: (206) 768-1990

Website: www.pioneerhumanservices.org

Services Provided: Transitional housing, employment assistance, financial literacy education

When to Apply: Before release and after release

Eligibility: Returning citizens

FareStart

Address: 700 Virginia Street, Seattle, WA 98101

Phone: (206) 443-1233

Website: www.farestart.org

Services Provided: Job training, employment placement, workforce readiness

When to Apply: After release
Eligibility: Returning citizens

Goodwill Industries of the Inland Northwest
Address: 130 East 3rd Avenue, Spokane, WA 99202
Phone: (509) 838-4246
Website: www.gwin.org
Services Provided: Job training, employment placement, financial literacy education
When to Apply: After release
Eligibility: Returning citizens

Catholic Community Services of Western Washington
Address: 100 23rd Avenue South, Seattle, WA 98144
Phone: (206) 328-5696
Website: www.ccsww.org
Services Provided: Housing assistance, employment support, financial counseling
When to Apply: After release
Eligibility: Returning citizens

Urban League of Metropolitan Seattle
Address: 105 14th Avenue, Seattle, WA 98122
Phone: (206) 461-3792
Website: www.urbanleague.org
Services Provided: Job placement, workforce training, financial literacy education
When to Apply: After release
Eligibility: Returning citizens

Northwest Justice Project
Address: 401 2nd Avenue South, Suite 407, Seattle, WA 98104

Phone: (206) 464-1519

Website: www.nwjustice.org

Services Provided: Legal assistance, expungement guidance, employment barrier removal

When to Apply: After release

Eligibility: Returning citizens

Seattle Central College Workforce Programs

Address: 1701 Broadway, Seattle, WA 98122

Phone: (206) 934-3800

Website: www.seattlecentral.edu

Services Provided: Trade certifications, workforce training, employment readiness

When to Apply: After release

Eligibility: Returning citizens

Seattle Housing Authority

Address: 190 Queen Anne Avenue North, Seattle, WA 98109

Phone: (206) 615-3300

Website: www.seattlehousing.org

Services Provided: Housing assistance, employment support, financial literacy education

When to Apply: After release

Eligibility: Returning citizens

King County Housing Authority

Address: 600 Andover Park West, Tukwila, WA 98188

Phone: (206) 574-1100

Website: www.kcha.org

Services Provided: Housing assistance, employment referrals, financial literacy education

When to Apply: After release

Eligibility: Returning citizens

. . .

Washington State Department of Social and Health Services

Address: 1115 Washington Street SE, Olympia, WA 98504

Phone: (877) 501-2233

Website: www.dshs.wa.gov

Services Provided: Financial assistance, housing support, employment referrals

When to Apply: After release

Eligibility: Returning citizens

State #48: West Virginia

West Virginia Division of Corrections and Rehabilitation – Reentry Services Division

Address: 1409 Greenbrier Street, Charleston, WV 25311

Phone: (304) 558-2036

Website: www.wv.gov/dcr

Services Provided: Pre-release planning, employment readiness, housing referrals, identification assistance

When to Apply: Before release and immediately after release

Eligibility: Individuals releasing from West Virginia state correctional facilities

WorkForce West Virginia

Address: 112 California Avenue, Charleston, WV 25305

Phone: (304) 558-7024

Website: www.workforcewv.org

Services Provided: Job placement, workforce training, apprenticeships, career counseling

When to Apply: Immediately after release

Eligibility: West Virginia residents, including returning citizens

WorkForce West Virginia Career Centers

Address: Multiple statewide locations

Phone: (304) 558-7024

Website: www.workforcewv.org

Services Provided: Employment placement, resume assistance, workforce readiness training

When to Apply: After release

Eligibility: Returning citizens

West Virginia Housing Development Fund

Address: 5710 MacCorkle Avenue SE, Charleston, WV 25304

Phone: (304) 391-8600

Website: www.wvhdf.com

Services Provided: Housing assistance programs, rental support, housing referrals

When to Apply: After release

Eligibility: Returning citizens

Goodwill Industries of Kanawha Valley

Address: 209 Virginia Street West, Charleston, WV 25302

Phone: (304) 346-0811

Website: www.goodwillkv.com

Services Provided: Job training, employment placement, financial literacy education

When to Apply: After release

Eligibility: Returning citizens

West Virginia Coalition to End Homelessness

Address: 1604 Washington Street East, Charleston, WV 25311

Phone: (304) 344-9000

Website: www.wvceh.org

Services Provided: Housing assistance, employment support, financial literacy education

When to Apply: After release

Eligibility: Returning citizens

Catholic Charities West Virginia

Address: 2000 Main Street, Wheeling, WV 26003

Phone: (304) 905-9860

Website: www.catholiccharitieswv.org

Services Provided: Housing assistance, employment support, financial counseling

When to Apply: After release

Eligibility: Returning citizens

Urban League of Charleston

Address: Charleston, WV

Phone: Contact local office

Website: www.ulcharlestonwv.org

Services Provided: Job placement, workforce training, financial literacy education

When to Apply: After release

Eligibility: Returning citizens

Legal Aid of West Virginia

Address: 922 Quarrier Street, Suite 400, Charleston, WV 25301

Phone: (866) 255-4370

Website: www.lawv.net

Services Provided: Legal assistance, expungement guidance, employment barrier removal

When to Apply: After release

Eligibility: Returning citizens

State #49: Wisconsin

Wisconsin Department of Corrections – Reentry Unit

Address: 3099 East Washington Avenue, Madison, WI 53707

Phone: (608) 240-5000

Website: www.doc.wisconsin.gov

Services Provided: Pre-release planning, employment readiness, housing referrals, identification assistance

When to Apply: Before release and immediately after release

Eligibility: Individuals releasing from Wisconsin state correctional facilities

Wisconsin Department of Workforce Development

Address: 201 East Washington Avenue, Madison, WI 53703

Phone: (608) 266-3131

Website: www.dwd.wisconsin.gov

Services Provided: Job placement, workforce training, apprenticeships, career counseling

When to Apply: Immediately after release

Eligibility: Wisconsin residents, including returning citizens

Job Center of Wisconsin

Address: Multiple statewide locations

Phone: (888) 258-9966

Website: www.jobcenterofwisconsin.com

Services Provided: Employment placement, resume assistance, workforce readiness training

When to Apply: After release

Eligibility: Returning citizens

Wisconsin Housing and Economic Development Authority

Address: 201 West Washington Avenue, Suite 700, Madison, WI 53703

Phone: (800) 334-6873

Website: www.wheda.com

Services Provided: Housing assistance programs, rental support, housing referrals

When to Apply: After release
Eligibility: Returning citizens

Wisconsin Community Services
Address: 3732 West Wisconsin Avenue, Milwaukee, WI 53208
Phone: (414) 290-0400
Website: www.wiscs.org
Services Provided: Employment assistance, mentoring, housing referrals, financial literacy education
When to Apply: Before release and after release
Eligibility: Returning citizens

Goodwill Industries of Southeastern Wisconsin
Address: 6055 North 91st Street, Milwaukee, WI 53225
Phone: (414) 353-6400
Website: www.amazinggoodwill.com
Services Provided: Job training, employment placement, financial literacy education
When to Apply: After release
Eligibility: Returning citizens

Project RETURN
Address: 2821 North 4th Street, Suite 427, Milwaukee, WI 53212
Phone: (414) 374-8029
Website: www.projectreturnmilwaukee.org
Services Provided: Employment assistance, mentoring, housing referrals
When to Apply: Before release and after release
Eligibility: Returning citizens

Catholic Charities of the Archdiocese of Milwaukee
Address: 731 West Washington Street, Milwaukee, WI 53204

Phone: (414) 769-3300

Website: www.ccmke.org

Services Provided: Housing assistance, employment support, financial counseling

When to Apply: After release

Eligibility: Returning citizens

Urban League of Greater Madison

Address: 2222 South Park Street, Suite 200, Madison, WI 53713

Phone: (608) 729-1200

Website: www.ulgm.org

Services Provided: Employment placement, workforce training, financial literacy education

When to Apply: After release

Eligibility: Returning citizens

Legal Action of Wisconsin

Address: 744 North 4th Street, Suite 200, Milwaukee, WI 53203

Phone: (855) 947-2529

Website: www.legalaction.org

Services Provided: Legal assistance, expungement guidance, employment barrier removal

When to Apply: After release

Eligibility: Returning citizens

Milwaukee Area Technical College Workforce Programs

Address: 700 West State Street, Milwaukee, WI 53233

Phone: (414) 297-6282

Website: www.matc.edu

Services Provided: Trade certifications, workforce training, employment readiness

When to Apply: After release

Eligibility: Returning citizens

. . .

Milwaukee Housing Authority

Address: 809 North Broadway, Milwaukee, WI 53202

Phone: (414) 286-8500

Website: www.hacm.org

Services Provided: Housing assistance, employment support, financial literacy education

When to Apply: After release

Eligibility: Returning citizens

Madison Community Development Authority

Address: 215 Martin Luther King Jr. Boulevard, Madison, WI 53703

Phone: (608) 266-4675

Website: www.cityofmadison.com/cda

Services Provided: Housing assistance, employment referrals, financial literacy education

When to Apply: After release

Eligibility: Returning citizens

Wisconsin Department of Health Services

Address: 1 West Wilson Street, Madison, WI 53703

Phone: (608) 266-1865

Website: www.dhs.wisconsin.gov

Services Provided: Financial assistance, housing support, employment referrals

When to Apply: After release

Eligibility: Returning citizens

United Way of Wisconsin

Address: Multiple statewide locations

Phone: (608) 246-4350

Website: www.unitedwaywi.org

Services Provided: Housing referrals, employment assistance, financial literacy education

When to Apply: After release

Eligibility: Returning citizens

Salvation Army Wisconsin Division

Address: 11315 West Watertown Plank Road, Milwaukee, WI 53226

Phone: (414) 302-4300

Website: www.salvationarmywi.org

Services Provided: Transitional housing, employment readiness, financial counseling

When to Apply: Before release and after release

Eligibility: Returning citizens

211 Wisconsin Reentry Support Line

Address: Statewide service

Phone: 211

Website: www.211wisconsin.communityos.org

Services Provided: Referrals for housing, employment, financial assistance

When to Apply: Before release and after release

Eligibility: Returning citizens

State #50: Wyoming

Wyoming Department of Corrections – Reentry Services Division

Address: 1934 Wyott Drive, Suite 100, Cheyenne, WY 82002

Phone: (307) 777-7208

Website: www.corrections.wyo.gov

Services Provided: Pre-release planning, employment readiness, housing referrals, identification assistance

When to Apply: Before release and immediately after release

Eligibility: Individuals releasing from Wyoming state correctional facilities

Wyoming Department of Workforce Services

Address: 5221 Yellowstone Road, Cheyenne, WY 82002

Phone: (307) 777-8650

Website: www.dws.wyo.gov

Services Provided: Job placement, workforce training, apprenticeships, career counseling

When to Apply: Immediately after release

Eligibility: Wyoming residents, including returning citizens

Wyoming Workforce Centers

Address: Multiple statewide locations

Phone: (307) 777-8650

Website: www.dws.wyo.gov/workforce-centers

Services Provided: Employment placement, resume assistance, workforce readiness training

When to Apply: After release

Eligibility: Returning citizens

Wyoming Community Development Authority

Address: 155 North Beech Street, Casper, WY 82601

Phone: (307) 265-0603

Website: www.wyomingcda.com

Services Provided: Housing assistance programs, rental support, housing referrals

When to Apply: After release

Eligibility: Returning citizens

Volunteers of America Northern Rockies

Address: 3322 Strahan Parkway, Sheridan, WY 82801

Phone: (307) 672-0475

Website: www.voanr.org

Services Provided: Transitional housing, employment assistance, financial literacy education

When to Apply: Before release and after release

Eligibility: Returning citizens

Goodwill Industries of Wyoming

Address: 619 East Carlson Street, Cheyenne, WY 82009

Phone: (307) 634-0898

Website: www.goodwillwy.org

Services Provided: Job training, employment placement, financial literacy education

When to Apply: After release

Eligibility: Returning citizens

Wyoming Rescue Mission

Address: 230 North Park Street, Casper, WY 82601

Phone: (307) 235-3000

Website: www.wyomingrescuemission.org

Services Provided: Transitional housing, employment readiness, financial literacy education

When to Apply: After release

Eligibility: Returning citizens

Catholic Charities of Wyoming

Address: 1500 East 12th Street, Cheyenne, WY 82001

Phone: (307) 637-9785

Website: www.catholiccharitieswyoming.org

Services Provided: Housing assistance, employment support, financial counseling

When to Apply: After release

Eligibility: Returning citizens

Wyoming Legal Aid

Address: 1813 Carey Avenue, Suite 203, Cheyenne, WY 82001

Phone: (307) 632-7200

Website: www.wyominglegalaid.org

Services Provided: Legal assistance, expungement guidance, employment barrier removal

When to Apply: After release

Eligibility: Returning citizens

DID YOU ENJOY?

Did you enjoy the read?
Let us know how much by leaving us a
review on Amazon and Goodreads.

ASSISTED PUBLISHING PACKAGES

Bronze Package

- Includes:
  - Cover Design
  - Editing
  - Formatting/Typesetting
  - Publishing Consultation
  - Price: $400

Silver Package

- Includes:
  - Cover Design
  - Typing
  - Editing
  - One Flyer
  - Formatting/Typesetting
  - Publishing Consultation
  - Price: $725

Gold Package

- Includes:
- Cover Design
- Typing
- Editing
- Proofreading
- Two Flyers
- Formatting/Typesetting
- Copyright Registration
- Publishing Consultation
- Amazon Upload
  - Price: $975

Platinum Package

- Includes:
- All-in-One Bundle: Typing, Editing, Proofreading, Formatting/Typesetting
- Cover Design
- Three Flyers
- Publishing Consultation
- Copyright Registration
- Amazon Setup & Upload
- One Month Promotion
- Amazon Setup/ Upload
  - Price: $1,200

Individual Services

1.Editing Services

•Proofreading: $100

•Manuscript Editing:

•0-60k words: $350

•Contact for a quote for manuscripts over 60k words.

2.Manuscript Preparation

•Formatting/Typesetting: We will prepare and arrange your book's text and interior for printing.

•Price: $100

3.Design Services

•Cover Design: $100 (2 free revisions, any additional revisions will be an additional cost)

•Promo Flyer: $25

•Custom Flyer: Contact for quote

4.Distribution Services

•Amazon KDP Setup: $25

•Amazon Upload: $25 (if you already have an account but just need us to upload it for you)

5.Other Services

•Typing: $300 for manuscripts up to 40k words (Contact for quote for longer projects).

•Copyright Registration: $100 + site registration fees.

U.A.D PROMOTION PACKAGES

Tier 1: The Basics Package

Price: $99

Target Audience: First-time or budget-conscious authors seeking minimal exposure.

Perks:

- Social Media Shoutout: 3 IG Story posts a week for a month.
    - Inclusion in Newsletter: Mention in the "Sponsored Showcase" section with a link to the book.
    - Digital Promo Graphic: A simple branded image featuring the book cover for the author's use (i.e. Available Now flyer)
    - Support Sunday Link In U.A.D FB Group: Book cover and link in Support Sunday post in group (x4)

Tier 2: The Spotlight Package

Price: $199

Target Audience: Authors seeking increased visibility for their release.

Perks:

- Social Media Shoutout: 3 IG Story posts a week for a month.
  - Inclusion in Newsletter: Mention in the "Sponsored Showcase" section with a link to the book.
  - Digital Promo Graphic: A simple branded image featuring the book cover for the author's use (i.e. Available Now flyer)
  - Support Sunday Link In U.A.D FB Group: Book cover and link in Support Sunday post in group (x4)
  - FB Group Promo: Book posted Monday-Friday in over 20 Urban Reader FB Groups for a month.

Tier 3: Maximum Visibility Package

Price: $299

Target Audience: Authors seeking an increased promotional push.

Perks:

- Social Media Shoutout: 3 IG Story posts a week for a month.
  - Inclusion in Newsletter: Mention in the "Sponsored Showcase" section with a link to the book.
  - Digital Promo Graphic: A simple branded image featuring the book cover for the author's use (i.e. Available Now flyer)
  - Custom Quote Graphic: 3 Eye Catching Quote Graphics that can be used on Social Media.

- 3 To 5 Character Visuals: Visuals of the characters in your book that can be used for promo.
- Support Sunday Link In U.A.D FB Group: Book cover and link in Support Sunday post in group (x4)
- FB Group Promo: Book posted Monday-Friday in over 20 Urban Reader FB Groups for a month.
- Paid Ad: We will run an Ad for your book for a month on a Sponsored Showcase page with a customized caption, targeting your book's audience to grow your readership.

OTHER BOOKS BY
URBAN AINT DEAD

Tales 4rm Da Dale

The Hottest Summer Ever

Hittin' Licks For The Holidays: Atlanta

Wet Dreams On Lockdown: The Nurse

How To Publish A Book From Prison

How To Invest In The Stock Market From Prison

First Summer Out With My Prison Bae

By **Elijah R. Freeman**

Despite The Odds

Despite The Odds 2

By **Juhnell Morgan**

Hittaz

Hittaz 2

Hittaz 3

Hittaz 4

Hittaz 5

Hittaz 6

Coldhearted

Coldhearted 2

Coldhearted 3

By **Lou Garden Price, Sr.**

Keep Me In Mind

A Hitman's Gift For Christmas

A YN'S Muse For The Summer

Wizdom: Forever Your Gangsta

Charge It To The Game

Charge It To The Game 2

Charge It To The Game 3

A Summer To Remember With My Hitta

Snatched Up By A Hitta

Santa Sent Me A Real One For Christmas

Wet Dreams On Lockdown: The Unit Manager

Thug Me The Right Way 2

Thug Me The Right Way 3

Seizing A Gangsta's Heart For The Summer

Yours For The Taking

Wrapped Up In A Hitta's Love For Christmas

By **Nai**

A Set Up For Revenge

A Set Up For Revenge 2

Wet Dreams On Lockdown: The Librarian

By **Ashley Williams**

Trickin' On A Heaux For Christmas

Homie Hoppin' For The Holidays

Wet Dreams On Lockdown: The Female C.O

Letters Of His Love

By **Telia Teanna**

The State's Witness

The State's Witness 2

The State's Witness 3

This Time Won't You Save Me

This Time Won't You Save Me 2

His Summer Side Piece

A Holiday Heist

Healing The Heart Of A Detroit Gangsta

Summer Vows With A Detroit Gangsta

The Promissory

The Promissory 2

A Gangsta's Last Kiss

What Do The Lonely Do At Christmas

Colliding Into Your Love

Kenzo Steel

By **Kyiris Ashley**

Stuck In The Trenches

Stuck In The Trenches 2

By **Huff Tha Great**

Melted The Heart Of A Menace

Wet Dreams On Lockdown: Lieutenant Grace

By **P. Wise**

Merry Trapmas

By **Mia Sky**

Thug Me The Right Way

By **DiamondATL & Nai**

Wet Dreams On Lockdown: The Counselor

By **Paris Iman**

Wet Dreams On Lockdown: The Male C.O

By **Tamyra Griffin**

Wet Dreams On Lockdown: The Captain

By **TN Jones**

Wet Dreams On Lockdown: The Warden

By **Shawnice**

Atlantastan

Atlantastan 2

Atlantastan 3

By **Chris Green**

IN The Streetz

IN The Streetz 2

IN The Streetz 3

IN The Streetz 4

IN The Streetz 5

IN The Streetz 6

Hittin' Licks For The Holidays: Charleston

By **Tron Hill**

Hittin' Licks For The Holidays: New York

Bandemic

Bandemic II

Bandemic III

By **Freshh Moneyy**

Regret Has A Name

By **Aleya Mishell**

Coming Soon From
URBAN AINT DEAD

Drill
The Hottest Summer Ever 2
THE G-CODE
Tales 4rm Da Dale 2
How To Build Wealth With Bitcoin From Prison
By **Elijah R. Freeman**

Despite The Odds 3
By **Juhnell Morgan**

The Pryce Of Loving A Boss
A Felon's Promise
By **Nai**

Julian Knox
By Kyiris Ashley

To Die For
By **Tron Hill**

Bandemic IV
By Freshh Moneyy

Regret Has A Name 2
By Aleya Mishell

BOOKS BY

URBAN AINT DEAD'S C.E.O

Elijah R. Freeman

Triggadale 1, 2 & 3

Tales 4rm Da Dale

The Hottest Summer Ever

Murda Was The Case 1, 2 & 3

Hittin' Licks For The Holidays: Atlanta

Wet Dreams On Lockdown: The Nurse

How To Publish A Book From Prison

How To Invest In The Stock Market

From Prison

First Summer Out With My Prison Bae

STAY CONNECTED

Follow
Elijah R. Freeman
On Social Media

FB: Elijah R. Freeman
IG: @the_future_of_urban_fiction

www.ingramcontent.com/pod-product-compliance
Ingram Content Group UK Ltd.
Pitfield, Milton Keynes, MK11 3LW, UK
UKHW020145250726
13967UKWH00002B/878